Looking Forward to Monday Morning

Looking Forward to Monday Morning

Diane Hodges, Ph.D.

THRESHOLD PUBLICATIONS
San Diego, California

Library of Congress Catalog Number 99-97571

ISBN 1-929412-03-7

Illustrated by John Speeter
Text design by Book Works, San Diego
Edited by Laurie Gibson and Nancy Lewis
Cover design by Kim Johansen, Black Dog Company

THRESHOLD GROUP
4991 Concannon Court, San Diego, CA 92130
858-509-1913 phone
858-794-4078 fax
e-mail: threshold3@aol.com

Visit our website at www.thresholdgrp.com

To my friend, Bill Warren.
Without your help I never would have
had the courage to pursue my passion.
God Bless you always and in all ways.

Table of Contents

Acknowledgments —

Thank you to the many school districts and businesses, named and unnamed, who contributed ideas to this book. It took me five years to finish this manuscript and along the way I made some very special friends.

A special thank you to the Austin Independent School District, Austin. TX, Van Buren Intermediate School District, Lawrence, MI, and Coloma Community Schools, Coloma, MI—the districts where I spent my educational career. The staff members there made every Monday a joy.

To my friend, John Speeter, who has been drawing cartoons for me for over a decade. He makes me smile, he makes me laugh . . . he is my friend.

To Jaye Pratt of Book Works, who had the courage to follow her dream and kept me on schedule. What a great friend she has become.

To my mentor and friend, Dr. Thelma Urbick, who was always there to give me courage. She didn't live to see this book published, but she is such a part of it.

To the three men in my life, who I love unconditionally . . . always have . . . always will . . . my sons, Marc and Jeff, and my husband and best friend, Gerry. And to my new daughters . . . Jennifer and Kristin. I am blessed!

Introduction —

Enjoyment, fun, laughter, recognition, appreciation . . . these are the things that we can't get enough of. These are things that contribute to the quality of our lives. These are things that we can contribute to our workplaces to help enhance our own lives and the lives of those around us.

I began to study this very important topic: appreciation. People are hungry—starving—for it. Recognition and appreciation for a job well done is a key motivator for employees. But many managers don't understand how powerful it is, and they often don't think about giving that recognition. A poll of 1,000 employees surveyed their workplace needs. Supervisors have great influence on employees' performance and a huge impact on their effectiveness at work. Studies have shown that people who enjoy their work are more productive and creative, in addition to experiencing greater job satisfaction. (*HR Focus,* February, 1993) The same survey was given to the 100 immediate supervisors, asking what they thought their employees' needs were. The results were eye-opening.

Workplace Needs	Employees	Managers
Interesting work	1	5
Full appreciation for work done	2	8
Feeling "in on things"	3	10
Job security	4	2
Good wages	5	1
Promotion/growth opportunities	6	3
Good working conditions	7	4
Personal loyalty to workers	8	6
Tactful disciplining	9	7
Sympathetic help with personal problems	10	9

(Dr. Kenneth Kovach, George Mason University, "People Performance," magazine, October, 1996)

There is also a correlation between the way employees are treated and the way they treat those around them. People frequently leave jobs when they don't feel appreciated, and are less productive prior to their departure. Rather than attending to the job at hand, they are focused on preparing their résumés for their next move.

I talked with a woman who had been a student in one of my graduate classes. She taught kindergarten and was truly a master teacher. I would want all students to start their education with her. In our conversation, I asked how her school year was going, and she said that she had left teaching and was now selling insurance. In shock, I asked why and she told me, ***because I wasn't appreciated.*** She felt that the principal and the parents didn't appreciate everything that she had put into the job, so she left. What a sad statement.

A friend of mine worked for a countywide educational service center. He had successfully written a large, competitive federal grant proposal that was awarded to the district. He expected and awaited the many *atta boys* that this accomplishment deserved, but they didn't come. He continued his professional pursuits and published a book for classroom teachers. Certainly that would get him the praise he deserved. But the acknowledgment was minimal. Then, one day, it happened! An event took place that drew great attention his way. Staff members stopped by his office all day, a long banner was hung in the hall, a blurb went into the office newsletter, and at last, the long awaited and hoped for occurred—the Superintendent stopped by to extend his congratulations. What had my friend done to warrant such attention and accolades? *He won the Super Bowl pool.* That's it! He won the football pool. It was on that day that he decided to look for another job where his professional achievements would be appreciated.

It is going to become increasingly important to retain good staff members, especially in the educational arena. Education is facing huge teacher shortages that will only escalate in the future. It is predicted that the U.S. will need 2.4 million new teachers by 2008–09 due to attrition, retirements, and increased student enrollments. That number increases to as high as 2.7 million when factors such as declining student/teacher ratios are factored in based on nationwide class size reduction efforts *(National Center for Education Statistics Predicting the Need for Newly Hired in the U.S. for 2008–09)*.

The teaching profession experiences a high turnover rate. Twenty percent of all new hires leave teaching within three years *(National Center for Education Statistics)* and in urban districts, close to 50 percent leave within their first five years of teaching *(Darling-Hammond & Schlan, 1996)*. In a typical year, an estimated 6 percent of the teaching force leaves the profession and more than 7 percent change schools *(National Center for Education Statistics)*. Creating a work environment that is fun and where appreaciation is shown is crucial.

Typically, those entering the workforce today do not feel the same level of commitment to their employers that previous workers have felt. HR directors share stories with each other about the creative, yet unprofessional ways in which people have left their jobs (e.g., sending their boss a cake with a resignation letter inside, sending the message via a singing telegram, or writing *I Quit* in the snow on the windshield of the boss' car.) You can even go to a website (www.Iquit.org) that will e-mail your resignation to your boss. In one of the districts where I worked, a principal faxed in his resignation after his first week on the job.

According to the Bureau of Labor Statistics, the average worker has about nine jobs by the age of thirty-two. Companies invest a tremendous amount of money in training their employees. They lose $20,000–30,000 for each high school graduate who is hired, trained, and then leaves—and the figure for college graduates is $40,000–50,000. People quit when they are unhappy, and when jobs are available, there isn't a need for them to stay in a job and be unhappy. Acceptance, recognition of contributions, and encouragement of personal growth help to create employee loyalty . . . and retention. As an administrator I wanted to ensure that the best educators stayed in our district and that the best would want to come there as well. I wanted to make my building the most joyous place to work so that my staff would look forward to being there and would enjoy their jobs.

Elements of a recognition and appreciation program include:

Staff members should be part of the development and implementation of the program.

I presented my idea for a Staff Recognition Program to my boss and four counterparts and it met with semi-acceptance: one of the men responded that we already showed our appreciation every other Friday when the staff members received their paychecks. But there is a huge difference between *compensation* and *recognition. Compensation* is what employees receive for the job assigned to them— it's money— financial. *Recognition,* on the other hand, is what they receive for efforts that are above and beyond. It is praise from supervisors, peers, or subordinates. It's non-financial. People want and need the compensation, but recognition of a job well done can be an even stronger motivator at work.

Before initiating the program I conducted a survey of the staff to find out how they wanted to be recognized. I then created a committee comprised of members from each employee group to develop and implement the program, and found that just including staff members in the process was a method of recognition in itself. You can provide structure by helping the group members set their goals, but let them plan the program. The program then becomes theirs and not management's. Likely there will not be much of a budget allocated for these activities, so this group needs to be one that will have creative minds working for successful outcomes on a shoestring. And although managers think appreciation has to be "budgeted," a thoughtful sincere, spontaneous expression of appreciation can be just as effective as one that appears on a spreadsheet.

Recognition and rewards need to come in a variety of forms depending on the individual recipient.

Each person is unique and because of that, the way we want others to treat us is not universal. It's not a "one size fits all." No longer does the saying, *Do unto others as you would have them do unto you* hold true. What holds true for you may not hold true for another person. Therefore, it is important to figure out what types of appreciation/recognition activities are meaningful to the recipients. So, *Do unto others as **they** would have you do unto them.* Giving recognition in a manner that is not meaningful to the individual has little impact.

"This is nice, but I would have preferred a cash award."

Some people are auditorily oriented, some visually oriented, and others kinesthetically oriented; these individual differences affect how each person likes to receive recognition.

Auditory —

People in this category want to *hear* the recognition—they want to have you tell them or somebody else about their achievements or accomplishments. I once made the comment to the staff that I would rather receive praise than a raise. Many people disagreed, but for me the rewards of the job were not monetary.

When I was an undergraduate student, a professor challenged me when he said, *Give three genuine compliments a day and your life will be greatly changed.* Well, I didn't believe it, but I was willing to try this as an experiment for a week or so. Wow—was I in for a surprise! What I found was that, until then, many compliments had remained in my head; I had never given them to the person. I love Ken Blanchard's quote, *Good thoughts not delivered mean squat.* So I made an effort to tell the person what I was thinking. What a difference it made in my life—and theirs.

It came back the other way when I was going to my high school reunion. I went to an affluent high school; however, I had made it into the school district's boundaries by one street, and my parents were not affluent. My classmates had gone on to be doctors, dentists, CEO's, and although I had a Ph.D., the title of "doctor" in my name didn't pay much. I just wanted to go to the reunion with dignity. An hour before it started I was still trying on the half-dozen different outfits I had brought with me. As I was walking out of the hotel a woman stopped me and said, *You look lovely!* Did that give me an air of confidence? Did I walk into that reunion knowing I had selected the perfect outfit? Oh, yes! That lady had no idea what a difference her three words made to me.

So I pass the challenge on to you: Give three genuine compliments a day, and your life will be greatly changed. Try it!

Be aware of how you deliver the message—there is more to it than just saying the right words. Communication studies show that

55 percent of any message is delivered through non-verbal communication, 38 percent by the way you say it (the inflection in your voice), and 7 percent by the actual words you use.

Visual —

To show appreciation to someone who is visual calls for physical items such as certificates, plaques, letters, cards, smiles, awards, memos, gifts, etc.

I worked with a wonderful man who was also very frustrating. Because I had such high regard for him, his approval and disapproval had meaning; however, he never learned to praise those who worked for him. I struggled to gain his professional approval, but giving compliments was not a natural part of his being. Yet it was the essence of mine. I once had prepared a report for him and when it was returned to me, *Nice Job!* and his initials were written on the cover page. I was ecstatic. I framed this page and kept it tucked inside my desk drawer. I worked for him for fifteen years, and those two words from him helped keep my spirits up through many challenges.

Kinesthetic —

Other people are kinesthetic and are more touch oriented. They need a sensory experience through physical connection and motion. They like to have appreciation expressed through a pat on the back, a handshake, or a hug. Dr. Virginia Satir, an internationally known therapist, said, *Everyone feels skin hunger through their lives,*

and unless that hunger is satisfied by touching, there's a vital void in the emotional make-up that's going to cause deep unhappiness. We all know that babies thrive on frequent stroking. Well, adults are no different. When they are not patted on the hand, embraced around the shoulder or hugged, they withdraw into themselves. I prescribe four hugs a day for survival, eight for maintenance, and twelve for growth. Choose the recipients of this form of recognition carefully so that the appreciation is not mistaken for sexual harassment.

The program should be visible to others—coworkers, community, customers, students, etc.

Be proud out loud. The program should be both public and published. Get notice of the recognition to as many people and sources as you can think of, e.g., cable news channel, notes home to the family, banners, newsletter articles, memos, etc. This gives the recipient recognition from people both at work and in the community.

Change the program frequently so that it's fresh with new ideas and activities.

The same thing over and over again becomes routine and starts to lack the luster. Keep the creativity alive so that it stays interesting —and fun. Make sure the activities are consistent with the organization's philosophy and goals, but try to keep things lively with variety.

The first section of the book focuses on Appreciation and Recognition Activities. The next two sections are filled with ideas for fun things that can be implemented at work to make it an enjoyable environment. Walt Disney's quote says it all. *You can dream, create, design, and build the most wonderful place in the world, but it takes people to make the dream a reality. People rarely succeed at things they don't have fun at.*

Many of the ideas in this book were implemented in the districts where I was employed, but additional ones were sent to me from other organizations. Use these suggestions to develop a program and an environment where everyone will be *Looking Forward to Monday Morning.* Drive your colleagues **HAPPY!**

Section I

Appreciation & Recognition

*An organization elicits
the performance it rewards.*

Chapter 1
Group Recognition Formal Activities

YEARS OF SERVICE AWARDS

Being a "veteran" employee gives certain bragging rights. With experience comes wisdom (as well as gray hair and wrinkles), and most employees welcome a symbol or recognition of years of service.

Not so long ago people worked for one employer for a lifetime, but for the most part, those days are gone. The prediction now is that people will change careers (not jobs) seven to twelve times. If that's true, having multiple years of service in an organization may become even more noteworthy in the future.

In an informal survey I conducted, the most common award given to acknowledge years of service was a company logo pin with the number of years noted. Other organizations chose these gifts, which carried the organization's logo:

- A sweatshirt
- A briefcase
- A watch or clock
- A pen and pencil set
- An acrylic paperweight
- A plaque
- A set of beverage glasses
- A beach cooler
- A beach towel
- A golden apple.

These awards are often given at a special recognition dinner, a beginning-of-the-year breakfast, or an all-employee professional development activity. Publish the names of the recipients in the staff newsletter, on the local cable television channel, etc.

Rose Boutonnieres

Another way to recognize years of service was suggested by a high school in which the principal gives the staff members rose boutonnieres during a designated week. On Monday, he visits the most senior staff members' work areas, welcomes them, and gives them their flower. Each day a new group of staff members receive their flowers (one to five years, six to fifteen years, etc.) until the newest staff members are given theirs on Friday.

Name Badges

Have name badges made for the staff that include the number of years of service/experience they have earned.

Employee Calendar

Make an annual employee calendar that showcases employees who have twenty-five or more years of service. *(Fulton County Schools, Atlanta, GA)*

ATTENDANCE AWARDS

Absenteeism is a universal problem for organizations. Even if you are able to get a substitute no one can replace the absent employee with 100 percent effectiveness. Awards for excellent attendance should be public and published. List the names of the recipients in the community newsletter, submit them to the cable channel, send certificates home with students indicating that their teacher had

 4

perfect attendance, etc. Define the attendance level to be recognized. Will it be based on perfect attendance? One day of absence? Other possibilities are employees who miss no more than a half-day of work during the academic year *(Clarkston Community Schools, Clarkston, MI)* or employees who have not used personal illness days during the year. *(Lapeer Community Schools, Lapeer, MI)*

Employee Attendance Recognition (EAR) Program

One school chose to implement an EAR program. Each semester, staff members are given attendance awards. Those who qualify may select the incentive award of their choice. The awards include:

- A letter of commendation from the principal for their personnel file
- Two weeks of casual dress
- A 45-minute lunch period any five days
- A reserved parking space of their choice for one semester
- Three days of early work leave
- A $50 warehouse order
- Three days of exemption from bus and/or lunch duty
- Exemption from two after-school or evening "special events." *(Fulton County Schools, Atlanta, GA)*

Other awards could be:

- A cash award for one day of sick pay or the cost of a substitute
- A gift certificate to an area restaurant
- Logo merchandise
  First year—Stadium blanket
  Second year—Golf umbrella
  Third year—Sweater
  Fourth year—Jacket.

*Those who qualify may select the incentive award of **their** choice.*

Staff Calendar

Create a staff calendar each month featuring a picture of a staff member who was recognized for his or her attendance the previous year.

Portfolio Page

Create a portfolio page for the recognized staff members to put in their Professional Portfolios. Include a certificate and description of the criteria for receiving the award. The Portfolio can be used in a performance review or as a self-esteem builder. It's great to review it on days when you wonder why you ever chose this profession. Then you realize what a difference you have made. *(See the form at the back of this book to order Portfolio materials.)*

Attendance Recognition Banner

Hang a banner displaying the names of the people who were recognized for outstanding attendance in a location that has a lot of traffic. *(American Airlines, Dallas, TX)* When I was in the airport in Dallas I observed a huge banner listing the names of employees who had perfect attendance for five-plus years strung across the terminal for all passengers to see.

Looking Forward to Monday Morning

RECOGNITION FROM THE BOSS

Being recognized and appreciated by those in the "head shed" is a nice bonus for staff members. It opens lines of communication and provides an opportunity to share success.

In-Touch Lottery

Have you ever found yourself saying, *I wish my boss would do my job for one day—just one day! Then he or she would appreciate me,* or *My boss has no clue what it takes to do my job!* Likely, we've all said something to that effect during our careers. Give some of the staff an opportunity to have their supervisors share their jobs through an "In-Touch Lottery."

> *"The farther you are from the front lines, the more you think everything is OK."*
> —Tom Peters

How It Works. At an event or meeting when *all* staff members are present, hold a lottery in which all supervisors' names are put in one container and all other staff members'

names are put in another. Select one name from the management container and one from non-management. The administrator selected spends a day (or half-day) assisting the staff person whose name was drawn in doing his or her job functions. For example, the superintendent may spend a day in the school cafeteria, with a teacher in a classroom, ride a school bus, work on the lawn maintenance, etc. Continue the drawing process until all of the names in the management container have been drawn.

Then do the reverse. Select staff members to spend a day with a manager to gain appreciation for what that job entails. Put the names of the bosses back into the container. Match the names of the managers with a new set of randomly selected staff members.

After the day together, have participants write what they learned about the other person's job, and publish their comments in the staff newsletter. This activity gives all employees a new perspective on how the organization operates.

Sue Conklin, Administrator, Paw Paw, MI, and Diane Hodges, Author

Principal for a Day

In conjunction with the Chamber of Commerce or other community organization, have various members of the business community serve as Principal for a Day to see the challenges that educators face. Participation in this activity also encourages the business community to contribute ideas and resources to address some of the needs observed.

Super Breakfast

Each year the superintendent ("Super") and administrators prepare and serve breakfast for the staff.

"Champagne" Breakfast

Customize the labels of sparkling juices with a motivating message. Have a "champagne" breakfast with the bottles on the tables for the staff to enjoy. You will find that many of them will keep the bottles as a symbol of appreciation.

Frozen Staff Meeting

One supervisor entered the staff meeting wearing an apron and carting a blender, frozen daiquiri mix, and plastic glasses. He made non-alcoholic daiquiris for the staff and thanked them for all their extra efforts.

"This Bud's for You"

Give each staff member a flower bud with a note attached. The note reads, *This bud's for you. Thank you for all your hard work.*

Library Lunches

Educators don't often have opportunities to go out to lunch, so one principal brought the restaurant environment to the staff. Arrangements were made for business representatives to cover the classrooms from 11:30 A.M. to 1:00 P.M., and the principal monitored all the rooms. The library tables were set up with candles and tablecloths, and a harpist was brought in to play relaxing music. What a wonderful change of pace for educators!

"Anything Goes" Meeting

Set a time when employees can meet with management in small groups to discuss *anything*. Urge the staff to be open with their concerns. Questions may be submitted in advance if desired. When the meeting occurs, ask questions that can't be answered with a simple *yes* or *no*. Make it clear that there is no penalty for candid comments and that honesty is welcomed. This is a time for management to express appreciation for the efforts made, too.

APPRECIATION EVENTS & AWARDS

Organizations have found a variety of ways to recognize and honor staff members, including:

- Holding a recognition breakfast with administrators where gifts are given
- Holding an appreciation event where hors d'oeuvres are served and gifts are given *(Sparta Area Schools, Sparta, MI)*
- Giving an award for an exemplary job at an all-staff meeting *(Allegan Public Schools, Allegan, MI)*
- Sponsoring an annual reception or dinner in the local area to express the business community's admiration for the people who help shape the minds of the students.

END-OF-THE-YEAR APPRECIATION

Had a "challenging" year—lots of changes, adjustments, etc.? Thanking staff members for their efforts is a good thing to do. Here are some ideas:

Chair Massages

During finals week or at the end of a project, have massage therapists come to the workplace. Schedule staff members to receive fifteen-minute shoulder and neck massages. Check with massage therapy schools to see if they have students who would be able to participate. One district used the profits from the vending machines to sponsor this activity. *(W.B. Travis High School, Austin, TX)*

Certificates of Appreciation

End a challenge-filled year with a gesture of appreciation. Make certificates for each staff member and present them at the last staff meeting of the year. Each certificate is personalized on the bottom by listing a "Random Act of Kindness." Recipients are encouraged to implement that activity to spread cheer to someone and to re-energize themselves. Examples include "Call someone you haven't talked to in years" and "Send a card to someone for no special reason."

Certificate of Appreciation

For making it through this changing
and challenging year

Patti Kenworthy

Thank you for being patient and realizing that
we are here for kids!!

Re-energize this summer and try this
"Random Act of Kindness" to spread cheer to someone.

Call an old friend you've lost contact with.

TEACHER RECOGNITION

New Teacher of the Year

The district selects a first-year teacher to recognize. In addition to a plaque, the recipient receives a plastic pancake. The first year of teaching is much like the first pancake you make—you don't serve it to company. The second one always turns out better.

Master Teacher Awards

Each year, up to five instructional staff persons with a minimum of seven years of service are selected for this award. The program identifies teachers who are recognized by their peers and the community as truly outstanding in their work with students and in their commitment to the district's philosophy. Recipients receive a stipend to use for conferences, educational travel, or curriculum supplies.

Distinguished Educator Award

Current staff members with three continuous years of service are eligible; two to five awards are given annually. The criteria used are:

- Professional skills
- Personal qualities
- Educational expertise and involvement
- Other service to schools and students
- Active and useful role outside of education.
  (Lapeer Community Schools, Lapeer, MI)

Teacher of the Year

Recipients are selected by their peers to represent their schools. A formal luncheon is held in the fall to honor these educators. Honorees receive a *Teacher of the Year* license plate, canvas bag, plaque, and a glass etching. *(Fulton County Schools, Atlanta, GA)*

Board Recognition

Each month the Board of Education acknowledges employees and schools that have received regional, state, or national recognition. They are first on the agenda and receive Certificates of Appreciation. *(Fulton County Schools, Atlanta, GA)*

Sabbatical Leave

Each year a full-paid sabbatical leave is provided to a member of the instructional staff who has a minimum of seven years in the district. The purpose of the leave is for professional growth and sharing of experiences and learning upon returning to the district.

ABOVE & BEYOND THE CALL OF DUTY

Extra Miler Award

In one school district, the Board of Education recognizes employees who do their share—and then go the "extra mile." Staff members nominate their colleagues for an Extra Miler Award on a nomination form that lists the names of all the previous award winners who are currently working for the district. Winners receive a framed copy of the Extra Miler resolution approved by the Board of Education, a cloisonné pin of the Flag of Learning and Liberty, and a gift certificate donated by a local restaurant. In addition, an article about the individual is submitted to the newspaper for publication. *(Plymouth-Canton Community Schools, Plymouth, MI)* **Note:** You could also make this the "Extra Kilometer Award."

A.B.C.D. Award

Staff members are honored with an A.B.C.D. Award for performing *Above & Beyond the Call of Duty.* Individuals are asked to identify the activities in which they're involved.

A.B.C.D.
Above & Beyond the Call of Duty

Staff Volunteer Service Recognition

The A.B.C.D. Award honors staff who volunteer to perform Above & Beyond the Call of Duty. Jobs and duties that carry a stipend (monetary or compensatory time) and extra duties directly related to paid jobs *do not* qualify for consideration.

Please check any of the following district activities in which you currently participate.

_____ Curriculum Coordinating Committee

_____ Computer Curriculum Committee

_____ Gifted/Talented Committee

_____ Writing Curriculum Committee

_____ Reading Curriculum Committee

_____ Substance Abuse Awareness Committee

_____ Community Education Advisory Committee

_____ School Improvement Team

_____ Public Relations Committee

_____ Other: _____

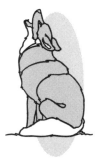

Timber Wolf Award

This is a weekly recognition of any staff member who has performed an A.B.C.D. act. Staff members nominate their colleagues by submitting a description of the noteworthy effort. An article about the winner is included in the daily staff e-mail bulletin and he or she receives a half-dozen huge chocolate chip cookies to share with colleagues. *(Traverse City Area Public Schools, Traverse City, MI)*

Red Apple Award

An award is given twice a year to employees who have contributed beyond what is considered to be their job. Award winners are selected by the superintendent, principals, and/or directors. They're given a "Red Apple" pin and are featured in a newsletter article.

Superintendent's Award

A plaque is presented to a staff member for outstanding contributions in the area of community-school relations. *(Marshall Public Schools, Marshall, MI)*

"Power of One" Award

An award is given to a staff person for making a difference in someone's life. For example, while I was giving a presentation for the Lake County, Illinois, Education-to-Careers program, the custodian told me he was a volunteer firefighter and had recently saved the life of a three-month-old child. If that district had had this award, I'm sure he would have been a recipient.

NON-EMPLOYEE AWARDS

There are many people other than those who work for the organization who deserve recognition.

Tea for Substitute Teachers & Temps

Substitute teachers are in such demand that recognizing and appreciating them is meaningful. One way to do this is by having a tea in their honor. *(Fraser Public Schools,*

Fraser, MI) Make them feel welcome and part of the team so they put your school on the top of their list.

Citizenship Award

An annual recognition is given at a Back-to-School community breakfast to a citizen who has provided exemplary service in support of a school district program. The recipient is given an engraved Golden Apple Award. *(Marshall Public Schools, Marshall, MI)*

VIPS Awards— Volunteers in Public Schools

The Board of Education and the "I Care Committee" congratulate volunteers who make a difference in the schools. They recognize those who are positive and pleasant, communicate well with staff and children, represent the district, are self-motivated, helpful, and consistently give a "100 percent plus" effort. Those recognized receive a framed copy of a resolution approved by the Board, a volunteer pin, and a gift certificate donated by an area restaurant. *(Plymouth-Canton Community Schools, Plymouth, MI)*

Outstanding Service Award

An annual Outstanding Service Award recognizes community members who have given superior service to a project(s). One individual is recognized from each school and receives the award at a Board of Education meeting. *(Clarkston Community Schools, Clarkston, MI)*

School Bell Award

Although the School Bell Award may be received by employees, it typically goes to non-employees who have rendered support and service to the district. *(Allegan Public Schools, Allegan, MI)*

Senior Citizen Appreciation

Senior citizens add so much to the community. Holding Senior Citizen Appreciation events for them is fun. Host a banquet to recognize seniors' contributions *(Fraser Public Schools, Fraser, MI)* or a high school "No Generation Gap" dance where senior citizens and high school students party together. *(Paw Paw High School, Paw Paw, MI)*

TEAM AWARDS

"Recognizing Our Success" Program

Employee teams are recognized with a plaque at Board meetings for activities that support the Focus Area of the district's strategic plan. Each month teams are recognized in one of the five areas, such as:

- Quality
- Diversity
- Mastery of Curriculum
- Student Learning Plans
- Community Involvement.

Weekly Team Awards

A small token award is given at each staff meeting to a group that has demonstrated team spirit. *(Traverse City Area Public Schools, Traverse City, MI)*

STAFF APPRECIATION DAY OR WEEK

"Everything Under the Stars" Luncheon

Hold a luncheon where the staff members dine under glittering stars suspended from the ceiling. Each star has a staff member's name imprinted on it in gold. *(Del Mar Union School District, Del Mar, CA)*

A Week of Celebrations

Hold special events to celebrate Staff Appreciation Week. Plans and preparations might include:

- Decorating the building with balloons and banners
- Giving flowers to each staff member
- Greeting the bus drivers at the curb with hot coffee, juice, and pastries
- Having a luncheon with music and culinary delights provided by parents and served by the students *(Del Mar Heights Elementary School, Del Mar, CA)*
- Sending a fruit tray or snack to each school with a token gift and a note from Board members *(Okemos Public Schools, Okemos, MI)*
- Giving out little "treats" each day of the week to celebrate the hard work and dedication of all the employees *(L'Anse Creuse Public Schools, Harrison Township, MI)*
- Giving a notepad and pen or other small gift to each staff member and preparing fruit and cheese trays for each school and worksite *(Kelloggsville Public Schools, Grand Rapids, MI)*
- Inviting a guest speaker to provide a motivational presentation to the staff. *(West Ottowa Public Schools, Holland, MI)*

Parent-Teacher Conferences Dinner

The itinerant staff caters dinner for the teaching staff during the week of conferences. The dinner is complemented by grape juice served in wineglasses. *(Traverse City Area Public Schools, Traverse City, MI)*

"Our Staff Is Magical"

At one school the theme of the week was "Our Staff Is Magical" and a magic show was presented as part of the celebration. Other events included an ice cream social, luncheon, and "magical" awards. *(Del Mar Hills Elementary School, Del Mar, CA)*

Board of Education Resolution

The Board approves a Staff Appreciation Day Resolution at its meeting. A copy of the resolution is sent to each employee with a cover letter of appreciation. *(Kelloggsville Public Schools, Grand Rapids, MI)*

Kelloggsville Board of Education Resolution

STAFF APPRECIATION DAY

WHEREAS, Kelloggsville staff are committed to the philosophy that all students can learn; *and*

WHEREAS, Kelloggsville staff support that philosophy by encouraging, motivating, and inspiring all students to achieve their very best; *and*

WHEREAS, Kelloggsville staff support each other in sharing their expertise and their interest in their students; *and*

WHEREAS, Kelloggsville staff support open communication among administrators, parents, teachers, and students to promote education in the district; *and*

WHEREAS, Kelloggsville staff prepare students for a global perspective in our rapidly changing world; *and*

WHEREAS, Kelloggsville staff are involved in solving educational problems that will lead to reform in education; *and*

WHEREAS, Kelloggsville staff actively participate in their communities; now, therefore, *be it*

WHEREAS, that the Kelloggsville Board of Education designates ___*date*___ as Staff Appreciation Day and calls on the citizens and educators in the Kelloggsville community to initiate appropriate activities to honor this important segment of our society.

School District Letterhead

Dear Staff:

Thank you for your loyal and dedicated service. Kelloggsville is a better place to work and learn because of YOU! You are an important member of our staff, and your interest in providing the best for our students is appreciated.

Sincerely,

The Board of Education and Administrators

Business-Sponsored Reception

Have businesses in the area sponsor a reception for teachers in the district to express their admiration and appreciation for the educators' work.

Catered Luncheon IOU

As an American Education Week gift for the staff, invite them to a luncheon. The meal is catered during one of the records days so staff members have time to enjoy it.
(Traverse Heights Elementary School, Traverse City, MI)

STAFF NEWSLETTER

Communication is the number one problem in most organizations. It's difficult to know everyone in an organization and be up-to-date on current events. Developing and distributing staff newsletters is an effective tool to acknowledge and show appreciation for the staff.

Intra-View

A one-page newsletter called "Intra-View" is published for school employees and provides information about birthdays, achievements, and current staff news. The reverse side of the page is called "The Flip Side" and serves as a communication tool for information from Board meetings and the central office. *(Marcellus High School, Marcellus, MI)*

Rapport

A monthly newsletter called "Rapport" highlights employees' travels, activities, awards, classroom teaching, special programs, and innovative ideas. *(Fulton County Schools, Atlanta, GA)* **Note:** Add the names of recent retirees to the mailing list for the staff newsletters. They'll love reading about what their working friends are doing.

The Coffee Break

A clever way to distribute your newsletter is to call it "The Coffee Break" and attach a tea bag or a small bag of coffee to it, which invites employees to have coffee while they read the current staff news.

Brew·A·cuP

Coffee Break of the Month

"Paycheck News"

An effective and inexpensive means of getting a communication to all staff is to include it in their paychecks. In my district we developed a brief newsletter called "Paycheck News" that is included in biweekly paychecks. It gives information on new staff, resignations, upcoming events, etc. There are sections for "Kudos" and "Did You Know That . . . ?" The newsletter provides an opportunity for staff to get to know each other better or extend thanks to others. Staff members submit information regarding their colleagues, e.g., *Did you know that _____ golfed a hole-in-one this summer?* or *A special thanks to _____* (a custodian) *for having the rooms look so great for the start of the year.*

Paycheck News

Our staff members have many talents, skills, and accomplishments that we often don't know about. To increase our awareness, this section will be part of the "Paycheck News." This will give you a chance to tell us about yourself or colleagues.

Kudos . . .

Your name _____

Name of person you're acknowledging _____

Recognition _____

_____

_____

Did You Know That . . . ?

Your name _____

Information to share _____

_____

_____

Chapter 2
Group Recognition Informal Activities

GENERAL RECOGNITION

Surprise Appreciation Events

Appreciation is more "appreciated" when it comes from the heart and not because of a date on the calendar. For example, secretaries like to be acknowledged for their contributions and not because it's designated as the annual "Administrative Professional's Day." Surprise appreciation events are effective for people who are often the "unsung heroes," those who work behind the scenes of successful organiza-tions, e.g., custodians and maintenance workers, secre-taries, crossing guards, accounting office staff, cafeteria workers, and bus personnel.

Surprise appreciation events you might try include:

- Making arrangements with a local salon, cosmetology school, or technology training center to provide office workers with an afternoon of pampering: manicures, facials, etc. My coworkers and I did this for our accounting office staff. We hung "YOU ARE APPRE-CIATED" banners in the offices while they were out for lunch. The staff members were in shock when they were told they had an afternoon away from the office and what they were going to do. They kept those ban-ners up for months. The reminder seemed to help on days when things "didn't balance."

- Bringing in a large submarine sandwich for lunch for all to share.

- Preparing breakfast for the transportation staff and surprising them as they get off the buses. When the administrators did this we notified the staff that there would be a meeting after the bus run. There was a real buzz as to what had been done wrong that warranted a meeting. When the drivers walked into the room, the principals were there to greet and thank them for all they do. It was a huge hit!

Dessert Day for Teachers

Have students' fathers dress in tuxedos and bring dessert into the classrooms. *(Fulton County Schools, Atlanta, GA)*

Looking Forward to Monday Morning

Appreciation Chalkboard

Place a whiteboard or chalkboard in a location where people congregate, e.g., by the elevator, mailboxes, lounge, restroom, etc. Title it "KUDOS." Staff can write positive comments about each other on it. OR . . . put a pack of Post-it Notes by the board and let staff write their information and stick it on the board. At the end of the week erase the board and start Monday with a fresh slate. Record the comments in a notebook to reflect on later, or type them up for the end-of-the-year review. They could also be included in a staff newsletter.

Examples:

- *Did you know that Karen ran a 5K race this weekend? Way to go!*
- *Sarah and Jack had a 6 lb. 10 oz. baby girl— Sawyer Marie. All are doing fine.*
- *Patti is at DAY 35 without a cigarette. Give her a well-deserved "Atta girl" when you see her.*

Office Laundry

String a clothesline across a wall and have a supply of clothespins available. Have cards and felt pens handy for staff to write notes of praise. Letters from students, parents, etc., can also hang on the line for all to read.

Lounge Bulletin Board

Designate one bulletin board in the staff lounge as a "Kudos Board." Have a supply of colored paper, markers, stickers, stars, glitter, and scissors available. Staff members can make items recognizing their colleagues and put them on the board. If there is a spare computer and printer in the building, put it in the lounge, too. It's great for making banners, certificates, etc., for the bulletin board.

Banners

If you have an occasion when many people are gone from their jobs for an extended period of time, e.g., summer or holiday vacations, plant shutdowns, etc., have "WELCOME BACK, STAFF" banners hung in the halls and elevators. You can also post messages on an electronic billboard.

I had a banner made with this quote on it for the staff's starting day in the fall:

**Education is the most important profession ...
through the hands of educators pass all professions.**

Match & Win Game

Obtain prizes from local businesses or other sources. Each staff member is given a copy of a U.S. bill ($20, $10, etc.) with the following note attached. Make sure you display the winner's name and the prizes awarded. *(Fulton County Schools, Atlanta, GA)*

Match & Win Game

Who Wants to Win?

The attached currency is for you—our hardworking teachers and staff. We wish we could afford to give you the real thing; however, you may be holding a winning bill!!

Look at the serial number on the front of your currency. Match it to one of the numbers listed on the poster on the door of the staff lounge and win that prize. Claim your prize by presenting your currency at the front office.

Good Luck!

Is this a winning number? Look to see!

All-Staff Photos

Annually take a group photo of the staff and give a copy to each member. It's wonderful to look at the photo and see members of the team all together. The photos also serve as an archive of memories as the years pass.

Department Photos

When the photographer is in the district taking student photos, make arrangements for photos of the staff in each department to be taken. Annually hang up the group photo in the departmental offices to remind all that a team is working together there. Keep all the pictures on display to provide a historical review of who was on the team over the years, labeling it "My, how we have changed!"

Buttons

Give teachers buttons with the message "Teachers Have Class" printed on them.

Annual Employee Calendar

Publish an annual employee calendar that showcases employees who graduated from a school within the district. *(Fulton County Schools, Atlanta, GA)*

Staff Lounge

If you make life on the job more pleasant, the staff will feel recognized. Providing a clean, comfortable environment in which to enjoy lunch and work breaks shows you care. Having a working refrigerator and microwave is a definite plus.

Smile

As simplistic as this may seem, a smile goes a long way in developing an environment where people want to come to work. If the boss is in a sour mood and doesn't appear to like his or her job, what can you expect from the staff?

The staff mirrors the boss' mood and outlook. Keep that smile on and share it often.

A study was conducted at Yale University in which the researchers tested appearance, personalities, and attitudes and their influence on others. They discovered that a smile is the single most powerful force of influence that we have. That's really great news, because we all have one.

Phone Smiles

Answer your phone with a smile on your face. It lets the staff know that you're happy to hear from them, even if they have a problem or complaint. Need to practice? Put a mirror by your phone and watch yourself as you answer it.

Listen

One of the easiest ways you can recognize staff and show that they're valued is to listen to what they have to say. Darlene Westbrook, my boss at the Austin Independent School District in Austin, Texas, is a master at listening. Whenever I entered her office, obviously interrupting what she was doing, she would put her work aside, turn away from her desk, put her hands on her lap, look me in the eyes, and focus her full attention on the issue I needed to discuss. It was the best gift she could give me—to respect what I had to say by listening to me.

Control your impulse to interrupt the other person with your own comments. Listen . . . truly listen . . . and then you can talk.

Smile For You

Smiling is infectious; you catch
    it like the flu,
When someone smiled at me
    today, I started smiling too.
I passed around the corner and
    someone saw my grin,
When he smiled I realized I'd
    passed it on to him.
I thought about that smile,
    then I realized its worth,
A single smile, just like mine
    could travel round the earth.
So, if you feel a smile begin,
    don't leave it undetected
Let's start an epidemic quick,
and get the world infected!
                    —*Source unknown*

"What Upset Me Today" Box

Instead of having a suggestion box, have a place where staff can express themselves and share what is not working in the organization by placing items in a "What Upset Me Today" box.

Casual Days

Dress codes loosened up in the early 1990s, and companies in Silicon Valley are credited with the movement toward "casual." Many of the CEOs were baby boomers, and blue jeans were standard dress from the time they were in junior high through college. Numerous companies have adopted dress codes that they term "casual days," "business casual," "corporate casual," or "smart casual." Companies vary as to how they have implemented this change in dress requirements. Some allow casual dress on Fridays, some on Mondays and Fridays, some in the summers only, and some allow it all days. I worked for an organization that allowed casual attire during the summer. That was really high on my list of employee rewards. A day without pantyhose is heaven.

The Aluminum Company of America (Alcoa), in Pittsburgh, went from using casual day as a fund-raiser to allowing it every day. Several years ago the United Way Committee asked Ron Hoffman, Alcoa's Executive Vice President, to approve casual dress for the duration of the one-week campaign for those who turned in their pledge cards early. Employees who turned in their

Bill Swain
Kalamazoo, MI

Today...

Employee "Dress-Down" Day!

cards on Monday had four days of casual dress, if they turned them in on Tuesday, they had three casual days, etc.

"We got almost 70 percent of our cards turned in on the first day!" Hoffman reported. "More importantly, people seemed to really enjoy the week more than normal, and in the days and weeks following the campaign, I got one voice mail after another telling me what a great idea this was, how much folks enjoyed it, and suggesting we continue it." Questions sometimes arise about what kind of guidelines staff members are given and who monitors them. Hoffman said that at Alcoa, "We empowered the employees to decide for themselves what the standards and guidelines ought to be for dress."

Alfred Posti of Alcoa adds, "We haven't had any problems with abuse of it. I think we're realizing more benefits than we originally thought we would," citing money saved on clothing and dry cleaning.

"I honestly believe most of our folks think this has boosted morale," says Hoffman.

The company my husband worked for observed casual day on Monday and Friday, and he loved not having to wear a suit and tie to work every day. One Friday he had oral surgery. By Monday he hadn't totally recovered and could have justified staying home, but when I asked what he was going to do he said he was going back to work . . . it was casual day Monday, and he didn't want to miss it. If you implement casual day(s) in your organization, you may find better employee attendance on those days.

> **66%**
> *Number of U.S. workers who wear business casual to work daily.*
>
> **58%**
> *Number of workers who say it boosts morale.*
>
> **(2001 National Businesswear Survey)**

GIFTS OF TIME

Time is a commodity we don't have enough of and it is often more valuable than money. Giving time off when needed is greatly appreciated. Time off to balance family and work is more important today than it was five years ago. What a difference it makes to get on the highway an hour earlier when traveling over a holiday or to be able to leave early to get to your child's play or athletic event or to attend a parent-teacher conference.

Early Release

Thank you for a job well done. This card entitles you to one hour of early release on a mutually agreed upon date.

_____   _____
Signature   *Date*

Early Release Cards

Early Release Cards can be given to all staff at the start of the year or used as rewards when someone does something worthy of recognition or acknowledgment.

Substitute Lotto

Each fall the names of the teaching staff are put into a container for a drawing. Each of the district's administrators selects the name of a staff person. As a show of appreciation, the administrators substitute for the teacher on a mutually agreed upon date, with no strings attached. Usually these days are used for Christmas shopping, the first day of hunting season, or the opening day of baseball season. When a teacher's name is drawn, his or her name is eliminated from the next year's drawing. Eligibility is regained the following year.

In a variation of this activity, each Monday morning the principal draws the name of a staff person and substitutes for him or her for a half hour during the week. *(Paw Paw Public Schools, Paw Paw, MI)*

Recess Pass

This entitles the bearer to "Pass" on Recess Duty for one day. Arrangements for coverage are to be made twenty-four hours in advance.

_____   _____
Principal   *Expiration Date*

Recess Pass

Once a year the principal gives each staff member a Recess Pass. With twenty-four hours of advance notice, the principal takes the teacher's recess duty. *(Traverse City Area Public Schools, Traverse City, MI)*

Looking Forward to Monday Morning

Movie Time

Students are gathered into the gym to see a movie and are supervised by the principal and parent volunteers. Teachers then have free time to catch up on things they need to do in their classrooms, develop curriculum, or participate in team planning activities.

Flexibility Pass

Have the principal give each staff member a half hour of her or his time. If the staff person needs to start work late, leave early, or take a long lunch, the principal covers the duties.

SPECIAL PEOPLE RECOGNITION

Sunshine Committee

Designate a "Sunshine Committee" to monitor and acknowledge births, deaths, illnesses, etc. Have all staff members contribute to the Sunshine Fund and have the committee send acknowledgments on behalf of the entire staff.

The Apple Sauce Gang

One morning after I had experienced a very tough previous day, I found a shiny, fresh red apple on my desk along with this drawing and saying. To this day, I don't know where it came from, but it certainly was appreciated.

A smile a day, keeps the students at bay. This apple today, should chase the blues away.

Be happy! We care about you.

The Apple Sauce Gang

SPC Committee

A group who called themselves the SPC Committee (Special People Care) made it their mission to help others when it was needed. It was an anonymous group to which each member contributed money for "hits." When someone had a death in the family, an unfortunate incident, etc., the committee would do something nice for that person. Here are some examples of their "hits."

MEMO

Date:
To: SPC Committee Members
Re: Emergency Hit

This morning we had an emergency SPC hit for Sarah. One of the students in the Auto Mechanics Program was to take her car from the parking lot to the program area for repairs. The student took it for a drive first and it ended up wrapped around a tree on Banger Road. Wouldn't you know, the tree just happened to be in Sarah's front yard. Luckily, the student was uninjured, but the car was totaled!

Because of this unfortunate incident we sent her a "Somebody Cares" bunny. This is an apology for not consulting with everyone, but it really was an emergency.

—*Special People Care (SPC)*

MEMO

Date:
To: SPC Committee Members
Re: Hit

This morning another hit was made. The recipient was Joe. As you know, Joe's mother passed away, so we thought we would cheer him up with a cheese Danish and the following poem:

Life can deal really rough cards,
Ones that are often quite hard.

We just want you to know
Your friends care for you so.

We'll help you try to deal with
*   your pain*
And bring a smile to your face again!

Our thoughts are with you in
*   all you do.*
Enjoy your treat, it's just for you.

—*Special People Care (SPC)*

NAME RECOGNITION

The Most Beautiful Sound . . .

When you get a new phone book, what's the first thing you do? Flip through the directory to find your name. We all learned our name at an early age and continue to enjoy hearing it spoken and seeing it in print. Some simple means of name recognition include:

- Greeting people by name
- Giving credit where credit is due and using the name(s) of those responsible
- When a publication is printed, putting the name of the desktop publisher and/or the graphic artist in the credits.

Names in Print

List all the employees in the district in a symbol of a school house or apple and publish it in your local newspaper or district newsletter. The people listed will love looking for their names. You may want to seek a corporate sponsor to assist in the cost of the newspaper ad.

Notepads

Make personalized notepads and give them to all staff members during American Education Week or at another appropriate time. (*Lapeer Community Schools, Lapeer, MI*)

Business Cards

Have business cards made for *all* staff members: secretaries, paraprofessionals, maintenance staff, transportation staff—*everyone!* This is a great project for students to practice using their desktop publishing skills.

Name of School District
64 Reasons for Our Success

Ellie Bean
• Taylor Dinkins •
• Wendy Harris • Lucy Sans •
• Aster Mason • Char Park • Jill Resse •
• Ray Davies • D. Jones • Zoe Thomas • Betty Zell •
• Al Franken • Jolene Cohen • William Flynn • Zoe Schafer •
• Sheila Carr • Betty Stone • John Fellam • Lucy Louis • Mike Smith •
• Hillary Evans • Della Fontonen • Patricia Bowie • Cindy Lanson •
• Tory Rosas • Sheila Pellam • Ally Black • Jeanine Pastor • C. Lawson •
• Joey Hays • Fran Isabel • Anne Everett • Ethan Miller • Bill Flynn •
• Randy VanMartin • Terry Hunnicutt • Katy Green • Sheila Sanders •
• Charles Amerst • Francine Lieberman • Lydia Amos • B.J. Hunnicutt •
• Shanille Burchet • Joseph Granger • Steven Thomas • Dante Feriante •
• Johnathan Tidano • Danielle Hays • Taylor Davies • Sandy Martin •
• Mary Green • Jill Green • Terry Wolfe • Hattie Nelson • Bill Lawson •
• John Tulane • Charlene Mark • Mia Lee • Louis Fortel • Tom Metzler •
• Suzette Wehunt • Sharon VanBuren • Jimmie Smith • Rebecca Ray •

FOOD REWARDS—YUM!

Free food is becoming a highly valued employee perk, so much so that employers are using it to attract and retain employees. This can get expensive for organizations with small budgets, but the use of food can still be an appreciated reward.

I was in the checkout line at an office supply store when an employee from a neighboring bagel shop approached the manager holding a large basket of bagels. She offered the manager free bagels for the store's employees. The manager said "No" to the offer. I was in shock because I know how people love to eat and it would have been such a nice treat for everyone. Here are some low-cost, food-related activities to use with staff. (**Tip:** *Don't turn down free bagels!*)

- Place a piece of candy with an attached note saying, *It's great working with you!* in staff members' mailboxes every two to three weeks.
- Decorate a cookie inscribed with *Super* _____ (job title).
- Have donuts delivered to the staff lounge.
- Have students or staff members bring in fruit to be placed in baskets for other staff members. Have the fruit sorted, arranged, wrapped, ribboned, and delivered.
- Each day of a designated week, treat the staff to snacks, e.g., cheese and crackers, vegetables and dip, cake and fruit trays, etc.
- Hold a "Make Your Own Ice Cream Sundae" event.
- On a non-payday week, put a Payday candy bar in each staff member's mailbox with a note of appreciation such as "Here's an extra payday for all your efforts."
- Designate one day a week as "Treat Day." Each person is responsible for providing goodies for one or two Treat Days each school year. Hmmm . . . would Monday be a good day for this? *(Marcellus High School, Marcellus, MI)*

Looking Forward to Monday Morning

Appreciative Sayings

Attach appreciative sayings to food items and have them at staff meetings, on staff members' desks, placed in their mailboxes, etc.

- **Starbursts**—*Bursts with energy.*
- **Peppermint Pattie**—*Get the sensation of learning.*
- **Chocolate kisses and hugs**—*Kisses and hugs to you.* (Traverse City Area Public Schools, Traverse City, MI)
- **M & M's candy**—*Marvelous and Motivated.*
- **Cupcakes**—*You take the cake.*
- **Berry jam**—*You did a "berry" good job.*
- **Cinnamon buns**—*Thanks for working your buns off.*
- **Juice box**—*Thanks for sharing your creative juices.*
- **Stick of gum**—*Thanks for sticking it out.*
- **Plastic wineglass filled with jelly beans**—*A toast to a job well done.*
- **Skor candy bar**—*You skored a big one.*
- **Red Hot candies**—*Our staff is RED HOT!*

Staff Recipe

Attach the following recipe to a food item, e.g., cupcake, cookie, etc., and give it to staff members.

Recipe for Making a Good (job title)

Blend together:	2 cups	Time and commitment
	2 cups	Dedication
Add:	1 cup	Warmth and sensitivity
	1 cup	Patience and persistence
Beat in:	1 cup	Energy

Sprinkle with a sense of humor & serve immediately.

SYMBOLS OF RECOGNITION

The Medium is the Message

Just as small food items can be used to send messages, other small gifts can serve the same function. Try some of these with appropriate notes attached. They can be handed out at staff meetings, placed on desks for staff members to find when they come into the office in the morning, put in their mailboxes, attached to their paychecks, etc. They can be given to the group as a whole or on an individual basis as the occasion arises.

- **Memo or notepads**—*That was a noteworthy accomplishment.*
- **Packet of aspirin**—*Thanks for your hard work. I know it's been a headache.*
- **Package of batteries**—*Thanks for your enthusiasm. You really energize the whole team.*
- **Snow globe**—*I know you're feeling snowed under right now. Can I help?*
- **Tape measure**—*By every measure, you're GREAT!*
- **Packet of pushpins or tacks**—*Great job. Your presentation was right to the point.*
- **Band-Aid**—*I'm sorry. I think I may have hurt your feelings, and it was not my intention to do that.*
- **Party whistles**—*We did it! Let's celebrate our accomplishments.*
- **Wrapping paper and bows**—*Thank you for all your efforts. We'll have this project wrapped up soon.*

Looking Forward to Monday Morning

WORDS OF THANKS & PRAISE

Verbal Pat on the Back

When you hear a positive remark about an individual, report it to the person as soon as possible. If you can't find him or her, use e-mail or voice mail. Don't miss the opportunity to praise someone in a timely manner. Be sure you send the compliment "up" as well as "down." Praise the individual, but also make sure his or her boss knows about the achievement.

> *Send the compliment "up" and "down."*

Tell-A-Thank You

Parents, students, and community members are encouraged to call in appreciation messages for all staff members. Volunteers answer the phones and operate the computers. All messages are entered into the computers, and employees are given their messages on Staff Appreciation Day.

Tell-A-Thank You
February 6th & 7th
Call 555.263.2117

Parents, Students, Friends: Take a moment to recognize those who have touched your lives. Remember the employee who always greets you with a smile . . . the bus driver who waited for you . . . the custodian who fixed your locker . . . the counselor who changed your class schedule . . . the administrator who helped you out?

Phone lines are open on the above dates to receive messages for teachers, administrators, secretaries, custodians, paraprofessionals, bus drivers, food service staff, and other school personnel.

Messages will be delivered on Staff Appreciation Day Friday, February 9th.

Bus Driver Sunshine Letters

Can you imagine being a bus driver and maneuvering a bus on snow and icy roads with 60 children behind you? Bus drivers deserve an enormous amount of thanks for what they do. Sunshine Letters printed on bright yellow paper are sent to parents. They are asked to write a Sunshine Letter to the bus driver when there is an occasion to show appreciation. The driver who receives the most Sunshine Letters each month earns a special award.

Sunshine Letter

If you know a bus driver who does a good job, please write a Sunshine Letter to the driver. The driver who receives the most Sunshine Letters each month will get a special award.

The Sunshine Letter could say something like this:

Dear Bus Driver,

Thanks for being such a good driver and getting my child to school and back home safely.

My child told me about the nice way you told those kids to stop shouting (fighting, picking on someone, etc.). I really appreciate the way you did that. It makes a difference.

Sincerely,

Parent's signature
Student's name
Address
Telephone

Paycheck Recognition

If your paycheck stubs have room for a message, take advantage of the space and praise individuals for their achievements.

All-Occasion Cards

Just getting to a store to buy a card is sometimes a major ordeal; yet I wanted to be able to send messages in a timely fashion. I made up an assortment of cards to have at my desk that expressed various emotions. Then, when an event occurred, I would put a card in a staff member's mailbox, attach it to a cookie, have it taped on the computer when he or she came in the next day, etc. *(See the form at the back of this book to order All-Occasion Cards.)*

Design-A-Card

Hold a contest in which students design the covers of a birthday and Christmas card. The winners receive $25 savings bonds. Have the Board of Education and administrators send these cards to the staff on their birthdays and at Christmas. *(Saugatuck Public Schools, Saugatuck, MI)*

Note: If you send birthday cards, be sure that you sign them rather than asking an assistant to do it. A personalized note makes a card even more special. One district put Christmas cards with the district's name printed on them in each staff member's mailbox. Many of the staff thought they were very impersonal and requested that the money spent on the cards be donated for food baskets for those who needed them. So . . . if you send cards, make sure they're personal and sincere.

Teacher-Grams

Give Teacher-Grams to students or as a fund raiser sell them for 5¢ each. Students can fill in their message of appreciation and return the Teacher-Gram to the office to be delivered to the teacher on a specific day.

Teacher-Gram

Name of teacher _____

Room number _____

Message _____

_____

_____

_____

Signed _____

Looking Forward to Monday Morning

Staff Appreciation Essay Contest

Students are invited to write an entry of seventy-five words or less on the topic "What a Staff Member Has Meant to Me."

A prize is awarded for designated grade levels (K–5, 6–8, 9–12), and the winning essays are read over the public address system. The essay entries are presented to each staff member with a designer cover during Staff Appreciation Day. Place copies of the essays in a display case for visitors to read.

Staff Appreciation

You Are Very Special . . .

The attached essay was written about you for an essay contest. The topic of the contest was "What a Staff Member Has Meant to Me."

P.S. . . . you'll love this!

"I Remember" Messages

Students often return to the school at Homecoming or just to say "Hi." Encourage them to send e-mail or inter-school messages to teachers they previously had in their education.

Coworker Coupons

Make "Employee Recognition Coupons." Staff members give the coupons to a coworker when they observe him or her doing something worthy of recognition. They write what the event was that warranted the recognition and present the coupon to the person. When an employee has collected a designated number of certificates, the coupons can be redeemed for a prize. Some examples might be:

    1 coupon = a free car wash
    5 coupons = a free manicure, a fast food
                  meal, or dry cleaning
    10 coupons = a dinner gift certificate or a
                   gift certificate for groceries

"We Caught You Doing Something Great"

In this school district, staff members are encouraged to observe their colleagues' actions and have them recognized in the monthly staff newsletter. They're asked: *Do you know someone who put in extra hours developing an innovative lesson plan? Or someone whose quick thinking helped avert a dangerous situation? How about a coworker who always volunteers to stay late, clean up, or serve on a committee? When you hear about something great that one of your coworkers has done, let us hear about it.* (L'Anse Creuse Public Schools, Harrison Township, MI)

Supergram

While visiting a university medical center, I picked up a Supergram. They're located throughout the hospital so patients, visitors, and staff can commend the hospital employees. The document is printed in duplicate so that both the employee and supervisor have copies.

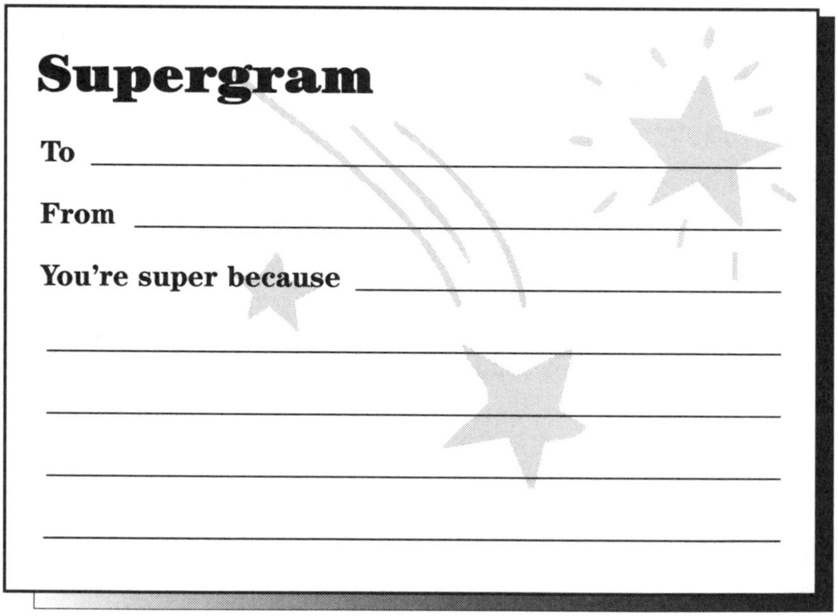

Supergram

To _____

From _____

You're super because _____

_____

_____

_____

_____

Looking Forward to Monday Morning

SOS—You're SomeOne Special

I am an avid fan of American Airlines. They send small SOS cards to frequent fliers who are in a position to identify employees who perform an outstanding job. The cards state:

> *When you experience an exceptional act of service by one of our employees, please take the time to present one of these "You're SomeOne Special" cards. . . . Not only will the employees you award the cards to receive your recognition of superior performance, but American Airlines will also reward them. By recognizing worthy individuals, you can play an important part in making sure the best employees in the transportation industry know we think they are special.*

I carry these cards in my planner and have found many occasions to use them. The joy on the faces of the recipients is wonderful. *(American Airlines, Dallas, TX)*

Employee name _____

Employee # _____

City/Base _____

Customer's name _____

AAdvantage # _____

Customer Comments for Employee

_____

_____

_____

_____

REWARDS FOR MEETING GOALS

School districts set goals for their staff: attendance goals, increased test scores, etc. Fun activities can be used as rewards for those who are working toward or have achieved those goals, whatever they may be.

Services Auction

Each person who qualifies by reaching the goal is given a sum of play money to use in an auction. The administrators designate services they are willing to perform for their staff, e.g., washing a car, babysitting for an evening, baking a pie, preparing a meal, an hour of yard work, etc. These services are auctioned off. It's fun to see how the staff members will pool their money and help their colleagues get the prize.

Administrators' Barbecue

The administrators grill lunch or dinner for the staff members to acknowledge a job well done.

Looking Forward to Monday Morning

Administrators' Car Wash

Have a staff car wash where the administrators wash the cars of employees who have met an established district goal.

Best Poker Hand

Use this reward activity with smaller groups such as grade levels or departments. With the group members, develop criteria in which they would receive a card, e.g. if they got their grade sheets in on time, if they had perfect attendance for the week, if they had over 50% parental attendance at the Open House, etc. When they have earned a card, each staff member draws a playing card out of a deck of cards that the supervisor holds. At the end of the designated time, the person with the best poker hand wins a prize.

Filling the Marble Jar

Develop criteria with the people who will be participating as to when marbles will be put in the jar. Examples might be, a marble will be put in for each person who has perfect attendance that week, for any note, call, etc. of praise that a person receives from a parent, colleague, etc, for each person who gets his or her grade sheets in on time, etc. When the jar is full, the group decides how they would like to celebrate—a pizza party, group movie outing, etc.

Chapter 3
Individual Recognition

GENERAL RECOGNITION

People like to be acknowledged for the effort they put forth. A word of caution, though—if the staff works in teams, giving individual recognition may be self-defeating. One school system implemented a "Teacher of the Year" program in which staff members were asked to nominate a teacher for recognition. No one was nominated because the staff felt they were all part of a team and either all members should be recognized or none at all.

Award Nominations

Nominate staff members for local, regional, state, and national awards and give them a copy of the completed nomination form. Whether or not they're selected as the award recipient, they feel honored to have been considered. Encourage the staff to nominate their peers for awards as well.

Adopt-An-Employee

This recognition requires that all employees in each school be identified and that selected activities are implemented. Parent-teacher organizations and students "adopt" a staff person within their building (not necessarily a teacher) and plan a recognition activity. Recognition could be a handmade card, letter of thanks, a poster depicting something special about that person, a special treat, an assembly where the students, parents, and staff honor the person, etc.

Random Acts of Kindness

At my school we performed random acts of kindness for each other during a designated week. We found that one of the best ways to maintain a happy and healthy attitude is to help someone else do the same thing. Not everyone was comfortable with performing acts of kindness the first time, so we published samples of what other people did for each other in the staff newsletter that went into the paychecks. Those who were reluctant the first time then had ideas of what they could do the second time the activity was conducted.

Random Acts of Kindness
Ideas from Our Staff

Gave an apple to Maxine Wilson for all the positive feedback she gives students and staff. —*Anonymous*

Bought a Butterfinger for Sarah Miles and thanked her for being a friend. —*Sally Kennedy*

Flowers were sent to a staff member whose wife had their first child. —*Anonymous*

Sent a thank-you note to Kate Murphy for the work she's done with the student portfolios. Kate has impacted many of our students and raised their self-esteem. —*Bill Banks*

Sent a note to Sharon Woods for all the extras she has done above and beyond her regular responsibilities. She always goes the extra mile. —*Anonymous*

Bought a dessert for a friend who was having company on the weekend. —*Shelly Thompson*

Sent notes to department members listing positive, descriptive words such as "good friend, supportive, professional, fun, forthright, etc." —*Loren Mendez*

I sent a supportive greeting to each of my students by loading clip art and a message on their individual computer disk. When they logged on to their computers, the message "Open This" was waiting for them. —*Mark Chan, Desktop Publishing Instructor*

Sent carnations to secretaries and bus drivers from the Foods Program at the Voc-Tech Center. —*Director of Foods Program*

Looking Forward to Monday Morning

Performance Evaluations

One way to recognize staff is through the performance evaluation process. Take time to describe and reinforce the positive things you have observed staff members doing and their relationships with others. The purpose of the evaluation is to facilitate growth, and it's an excellent opportunity to let employees know that you're aware of what they're doing and how much it's appreciated. *(Traverse Heights Elementary School, Traverse City, MI)*

SPECIAL RECOGNITION

"This is Your Day"

Designate a day to acknowledge one special person, e.g., "John Drenth Day." Hang banners, send notes from the staff, decorate with balloons, send e-mail messages, serve cake, etc. A standing ovation is wonderful if the whole staff is together. Our staff did this for the computer technician in our building. Everyone appreciated the help they received with their computers and wanted to let him know that.

Award Certificates

Make award certificates for staff and students who have done something special. Read the message on the award during the daily announcements. At Traverse Heights Elementary these awards are called "Traverse Heights Trophies." *(Traverse Heights Elementary School, Traverse City, MI)*

Heroes Bulletin Board

Create a large bulletin board in the hall that features children and staff members who have done something

special for the school. Title it with the name of the school followed by "Heroes," e.g., "Heights Heroes." Keep a disposable or digital camera handy and try to catch people doing something good. Post their pictures and a brief explanation of what they did on the Heroes Bulletin Board. (*Traverse Heights Elementary School, Traverse City, MI*)

Treasure Chest

Stock a treasure chest with items donated by local businesses and make keys out of construction paper. When you see someone doing something worthy of recognition, write on the key what the deed was and give him or her a "key" to the treasure chest. The person being recognized presents the key to the keeper of the chest (usually the boss) and selects a "treasure." Items in the chest might include movie passes, car wash coupons, dinner certificates, and so forth.

Member Spotlight

Have a staff person spotlighted in a communication that goes to all staff, e.g., newsletter or notices in paycheck envelopes. How do you select the person to be featured without showing favoritism? You could:

- Hold a random drawing from a list of all the organization's employees
- Ask people who win drawings or prizes awarded by the district to submit background information on themselves to put in a communication
- Feature people who reach certain levels of service, e.g., ten years, fifteen years, etc.

Employee of the Month

Each month acknowledge a staff person's contributions to the organization by publishing an article about him or her in area newspapers. To avoid favoritism, a community group could sponsor the recognition and select the staff people to be honored. *(Paw Paw High School, Paw Paw, MI)*

Employee Place Mats

As part of Employee Appreciation Week, have place mats printed displaying pictures of staff members representing each of the employee groups, e.g., teachers, transportation staff, custodial staff, etc. Ask the different groups to select one person to represent them. Distribute the place mats to area restaurants.

The place mats may also be used to feature staff members who have received awards throughout the year. *(Farmington Public Schools, Farmington, MI)*

Compliment Corner

Designate a showcase in the hall as "The Compliment Corner" so it can be viewed by staff, students, and visitors. Each quarter, recognize staff members by displaying pictures of them on the job and highlighting their contributions. When the display case is changed, the documents can go to the staff persons for inclusion in their Professional Portfolios.

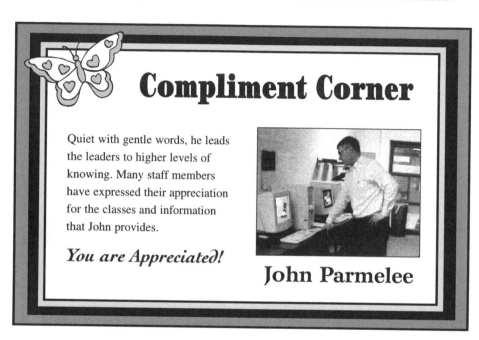

Compliment Corner

Quiet with gentle words, he leads the leaders to higher levels of knowing. Many staff members have expressed their appreciation for the classes and information that John provides.

You are Appreciated!

John Parmelee

Personal Profiles

List the names of all staff members on the left side of a piece of paper. Duplicate the page and distribute it to each person. Instruct them to write a positive statement about each of their colleagues next to his or her name, e.g., why they like working with that person, the qualities he or she brings to the organization, the characteristics the person demonstrates that other people respect, etc. Collect and compile the statements about each individual on a summary sheet and give it to the subject person. The sheet is an affirming reference that employees can review on down days. *(Texas Commission on Volunteerism and Community Service, Austin, TX)*

Looking Forward to Monday Morning

 Allen Dietz

Our Doppler, Interactive Traffic-Reporting, Resource King

Comments from coworkers:

- King of e-mail, encouraging, committed to service
- Steady, organized, knowledgeable, and eager to help with extraneous tasks
- The Commission Mr. Fix-It, always has whatever is needed to fix what broke, what tore, what hurts . . . whatever
- Eager to share his knowledge, eager to help others, acknowledges his strengths and weaknesses equally
- Impressive training capabilities
- Good listener, open, supportive
- Our most resourceful staff member
- Has invaluable skills as a communicator, very insightful in analyzing problems
- Equally outgoing and sharing spirit, very thorough
- Has a wonderful calmness, cheerful. He's the greatest!
- Always on the go! Disaster specialist, man of many resources and talents
- Creative, adventurous, loyal

> *A great document for your Professional Portfolio!*

Lifesaver Appreciation

You never realize how valuable and essential people are to an organization until they go on vacation. This idea was reinforced when the administrative assistant in my department went to Florida for two weeks. I don't remember her ever previously taking a full week off in the twenty years we worked together. Mainly, she took long weekends, and I could survive without her for two days.

I had always appreciated her, but when she was gone for two weeks, I *really* appreciated her. I recruited help from every assistant

> *Thanks, you were a lifesaver!*

in the building to fill in. By the end of the vacation period, the other assistants were as happy to see her return as I was. I made Life Saver chains for each of them by stringing rolls of Life Savers on a ribbon. At the end of the ribbon I attached a card that said, "Thanks, you were a lifesaver!"

When the assistant returned from her vacation, I posted a sign on her computer screen that read, "Welcome Back. You were missed!" (And indeed she was!)

A Hug and a Mug

Give staff members a hug and a coffee mug with an inspirational saying on it when they have done something worthy of appreciation. You can do this throughout the year or during the third week in June, when it's "Hug Holiday Week."

Halfway There

I often feel guilty about the amount of work that is passed on to administrative assistants. The pile seems to grow higher and higher. Sometimes when I had a large stack of papers, such as a grant application, for the clerical person to process, I would slip a candy bar, package of microwave popcorn, change for the soda pop machine, etc., in the middle. With it was a note saying, "Halfway There!! Take a Break." It's a nice surprise and helps to lighten the load.

Candy Bar

WRITTEN PRAISES

Everybody Needs Validation

Use "validation notes" to show appreciation for an act of kindness or to recognize something good that a person is doing on the job. All staff can use the notes and all staff can receive Validation Notes from any individual. *(Marcellus High School, Marcellus, MI)*

A Pat on the Back

Trace your hand on a piece of paper and have it made into notecards with "A Pat on the Back for YOU!" printed on them. Write a note of appreciation to someone.

A Pat on the Back for YOU!

A Matter of "Principal"

At one school, the principal makes a practice of sending complimentary notes and thank-you messages when the staff does something well or beyond the call of duty. For example, one teacher took his snowblower to the home play-off football game following a blizzard. It came in very handy. On Monday morning, he had a nice note from the principal waiting in his mailbox. *(Jim Carey, Paw Paw, MI)*

"Praise-Wordy"

Do you search for just the right words of praise to use in your notes to others? Here is a list, but make sure you identify what the outcome of the effort was. The words alone don't have as much meaning as when they're attached to a description of the act that prompted them.

Applause! Applause!   Bravo
Awesome   Congratulations

Exactly right	Right on target
Excellent	Sensational
Fabulous	Super
Fantastic	Superb
Good for you	Terrific
Good job	That's great
Good work	Thumbs-up
Keep going	Tremendous
Keep it up	Way to go!
Marvelous	Well done
Nice job	Wonderful
Now you have it!	Wow!
Outstanding	You did it!
Perfect	You did it this time!

Do you need help with words that describe the positive traits of the people you're recognizing? Here are a few:

Appreciative	Independent
Assertive	Inspirational
Capable	Intelligent
Considerate	Kind
Consistent	Knowledgeable
Cooperative	Loyal
Creative	Motivating
Dedicated	Organized
Determined	Patient
Disciplined	Persistent
Energetic	Positive
Enthusiastic	Self-controlled
Ethical	Sincere
Flexible	Special
Forgiving	Supportive
Friendly	Talented
Fun	Team Player
Hardworking	Trusting
Helpful	Understanding
Humorous	Unique

Student Satisfaction

Publicly acknowledge letters to educators from *"satisfied customers"*—the students. Have these letters printed in your local or district newspapers or newsletters. Provide a picture of the staff member for an even greater effect. These articles are great additions to their Portfolios as well.

Recognition should be "public" and "published."

Make It Personal

Print notepaper on carbonless paper to be used by the principal and supervisors to send personalized notes of recognition. The original goes to the staff member and the copy goes into the files. *(Frankfort/Elberta Area Schools, Frankfort, MI)*

Date:
To:

Effective Teaching Makes A Difference

Thanks!
Signed:

The Teachers Behind the Students

When a student receives an award or recognition, it's often written about in the newspaper. Include a list of teachers the student has had who contributed to this success.

Letters to the Editor

When parents or customers praise the way something is done, ask them to write a letter to the editor of the newspaper. Include the names of the people who contributed positively to this situation.

"Credit" Cards

Make cards that give credit where credit is due. When appropriate they can be given personally to the individuals or placed in their workstation or mailbox. Keep a stack of them handy so the recognition is given in a timely fashion. *(See the form at the back of this book to order "Credit" Cards.)*

TRYING NEW THINGS . . . GOOD & BAD

There are times when things don't go quite as planned, and you just don't want to hear about it from your boss. Failure is about "learning" and "trying," and all learning lends itself to some failure. Creating an environment where new ideas and risk taking are encouraged and recognized is beneficial. Employees are much happier in environments where occasional mistakes are allowed and not met with criticism or anger.

> *"To swear off making mistakes is easy. All you have to do is swear off having ideas."*
> —Leo Burnett

"I Blew It" Cards

Staff members are encouraged to be innovative—to try new things. People often have a fear of failure and find comfort in maintaining the status quo. Annually, the superintendent in this district gives each staff member an "I Blew It" card that allows him or her to try new things without fear of ridicule. *(Farmington Public Schools, Farmington, MI)*

I Blew It !?

I tried something new and innovative and it didn't work as well as I wanted.

Farmington Public Schools

This card entitles me to be free of criticism for my efforts. I'll continue to pursue ways to help our district be successful.

I was a middle school counselor during my early twenties. Each year staff members set professional goals and one of mine was to increase communications with the parents of the students in our school. I remember writing a letter to the parents of one of the students after report cards were issued. The letter went something like this:

> *Sarah is an outstanding student. Her grades are exemplary and all the teachers enjoy having her in their classes. You must be as proud of her as we are. She has such a marvelous future ahead of her in the years to come.*

A few days later I received a letter of reply:

> *I am very proud of Sarah, and I am happy to know that she is doing so well in school. She really seems to be held in high regard by the school. However, my daughter's name is Sally, and I was wondering if you could tell me how she is doing in school.*

Well, I wanted to just die. I never told my principal about these letters, and apparently the parents didn't either. I certainly made sure I never made that mistake again. I would have used my "I Blew It" card for this one if the parents had called the principal.

Enter-Prize

Establish an "Enter-Prize," which recognizes creative ideas that work. Have a prize for the successful suggestions that were implemented during the year.

Section II

Fun Ways to Spend Work Days

*People rarely succeed
at things they don't have fun at.*
—Walt Disney

Chapter 4
From the Beginning

NEW YEAR STARTERS

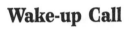

September is the start of the "new year" for most schools. Why not start it with one or more of these fun activities that give coworkers a chance to reconnect? These ideas have worked for other schools and organizations and might for yours as well.

Wake-up Call

Do you have trouble getting up to go to work in the morning? Log onto www.mrwakeup.com and have them call to wake you. You can record messages, music, etc., to start your day. It would be fun to record messages to wake up a coworker, too.

Retreat Treat

Take the staff on an overnight retreat. Ask local businesses, including the resort, to donate the facilities and door prizes. Every staff member gets a "goodie bag," and additional prizes are raffled off every hour. There is a huge amount of work accomplished at the retreat, but the staff also has a wonderful time bonding. New staff members start the year feeling as though they belong, and veterans feel recommitted to their jobs and to their peers. *(Traverse Heights Elementary School, Traverse City, MI)*

R$_X$ for a Good Year

Give staff members a medicine bottle filled with jelly beans in various colors and flavors prescribed for the treatment of "budget-itis, phone call ear, no time to sleep, busy day blues," and to help them maintain a positive attitude.

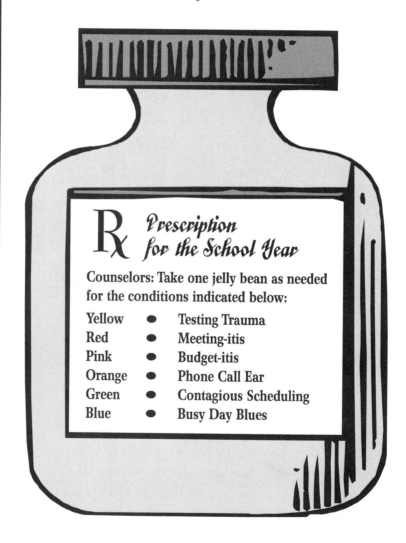

R$_X$ *Prescription for the School Year*

Counselors: Take one jelly bean as needed for the conditions indicated below:

Yellow	●	**Testing Trauma**
Red	●	**Meeting-itis**
Pink	●	**Budget-itis**
Orange	●	**Phone Call Ear**
Green	●	**Contagious Scheduling**
Blue	●	**Busy Day Blues**

Looking Forward to Monday Morning

Survival Kit

Make a Survival Kit for each staff member by placing the following "instructions" in a plastic bag along with the items called for.

Survival Kit for Everyday Use

Toothpick: To remind you to *pick out the good qualities* in others.

Rubber Band: To remind you to be *flexible.* Things might not always go the way you want, but they will work out.

Band-Aid: To remind you to *heal hurt feelings,* yours or someone else's.

Pencil: To remind you to *list your blessings* every day.

Eraser: To remind you that *everyone makes mistakes,* and it's OK!

Chewing Gum: To remind you to *stick with it* and you can accomplish anything.

Mint: To remind you that *you are worth a mint.*

Candy Kiss: To remind you that *everyone needs a kiss or hug* every day.

Tea Bag: To remind you to *relax daily* and *go over that list of your blessings.*

Source Unknown

You can give the kit to the staff all at once or by adding an item each week.

"What Did You Do This Summer?" Scavenger Hunt

Staff members are eager to catch up on what others did during the summer or during an extended period of time away from work. It's fruitless to go on with the business at hand until they've had this socialization time. Why not assist in this process by having a scavenger hunt?

Use the sheet below or develop your own, specific to your geographic area and interests. Give each staff member a form and ask them to mingle with their colleagues to find a person who did each of the activities listed and have them sign the appropriate square.

When it appears the forms have been completed, ask everyone to return to their seats. Go through each question, asking staff members who they found in each category. For

What did you do this summer? Find someone who . . .

Went Fishing	Worked Another Job	Ate Blueberry Pie	Learned Something New	Jogged	Rented 3 or More Videos
————	————	————	————	————	————
Saw a Great Movie	Read 3 or More Books	Swam in a Lake	Played Golf	Had Quality Time with Children	Grilled Something Outside
————	————	————	————	————	————
Traveled Abroad	Rode a Roller Coaster	Cooked Dinner 3 x a Week	Got a Massage	Mowed the Lawn	Went Sailing
————	————	————	————	————	————
Went Camping	Slept Late a Lot	Was Creative (how?)	Lost Weight	Surfed the Internet	None of the Above, but I Did:
————	————	————	————	————	————

Looking Forward to Monday Morning

example, *Who went fishing this summer?* Participants then identify all the people who have signed their names in that box.

Two Truths and a Lie

Divide the large group into smaller groups of five or six members each. Ask each person to tell, with conviction, two truths and a lie about _____ (e.g., How they spent their summer vacation, what they did over the holidays, what they do for fun, or any other topic of their choice). Examples in response to *What I did over the summer* might be:

- *I cooked dinner for my family every night during the month of July.* (lie)
- *I attended my son's high school graduation where he was selected as class salutatorian.* (truth)
- *I attended the Colorado Outward Bound program for three weeks and climbed a 13,000-foot mountain.* (truth)

Other members of the group have to guess which are the truths and which is the lie.

With the whole group, conduct a "Lie Off." Have each of the smaller groups select the most interesting, convincing person to share his or her three items.

Goodie Bags and Gifts

Obtain donated items from area businesses and have "Goodie Bags" waiting at each staff member's workstation. The items don't have to be expensive; they can be cute things such as small first aid kits, pencils, key chains, fast food gift certificates, etc.

Purchase logo-engraved items for staff members and disseminate them at an all-staff breakfast or meeting. Examples might include a memo cube, writing portfolio, etc. Giving people items they can use on the job is beneficial for all.

Your School's Name

New Year's Invitation

Send your staff an invitation to celebrate the beginning of a new year/school year. The invitation may also include the agenda for the first day back. Patti Kenworthy, a Hospitality Services instructor in Lawrence, Michigan, mails her students this invitation at the start of the school year. The free gift the students receive is a plastic sipper cup and straw donated by an area business. Her business card, a pencil, key chain, etc., are inside. Soda pop is provided for students to fill their cups with as they celebrate the start of a new school year. *(Patti Kenworthy, Stevensville, MI)*

You're Invited!!

To Celebrate the New Year

When: **August 25**

Where: **Tech Center, Hospitality Services**

Time: **8:30 a.m. and Noon**

Dress: **Casual and Comfortable**

BYOP—Bring Your Own Pen or Pencil

Return this invitation and receive a free gift.

See you then,
Ms. K

Thought for the Week

Type inspiring, motivational quotes on small strips of colored paper. Put them in a ribboned jar. At the start of the year, give each staff person a jar for his or her desk. On Monday, they select a quote from their jars to reflect on for the week. Here's a starter list:

- People may not remember what you do, but they will remember how you treated them.

- When you're through learning, you're through.
  —*Vernon Law, pitcher, Pittsburgh Pirates*

- The prospects never looked brighter.
  The problems never looked tougher.
  And those who are not stirred by
  both of those statements are probably
  too tired to be much use in the years ahead.

- A true commitment is a heartfelt promise to yourself from which you will not back down.

- Good thoughts not delivered mean squat.
  —*Ken Blanchard*

- Give to the world the best you can, and the best will come back to you.

- The most important "things" in life are not "things."
  Love people and use things.

- Life is 10% what happens to me and 90% how I react to it.
  —*Charles Swindoll*

- I am not what you think I am, I am what I think I am.

- If there is something that you wish to do, begin.
  There is MAGIC in MOTION!

- Imagination is more important than knowledge.

- Laughter is contagious. Start an epidemic!

- No one is perfect. That's why pencils have erasers.

- In the long run, the pessimist may be proven right, but the optimist has a better time on the trip.

- The most wasted day of all is the day on which we have not laughed.

- People know you for what you've done, not for what you plan to do.

- Doing for others always pays dividends.

- The six most important words: "I admit that I was wrong."

- Decide on what you think is right, and stick to it. —*George Eliot*

- People may fail many times, but they aren't failures until they begin to blame somebody else.

- Sticks and stones may break my bones, but words cause permanent damage.

- Do more than you're supposed to do and you can have or be or do anything you want.

- Remember . . . if you're suffering from burnout, at some time you must have been on fire.

- Three things in human life are important: The first is to be kind. The second is to be kind. And the third is to be kind. —*Henry James*

- A sense of humor can help you overlook the unattractive, tolerate the unpleasant, cope with the unexpected, and smile at the unbearable.

- If you don't like something in your life—change the way you think about it.

- If you can't whistle on your way to work, you don't belong in that job.

- If you want something, ask for it. —*Jack Canfield*

- If you can't have what you want, want what you have.

Looking Forward to Monday Morning

Secret Pals

Participating staff members have "Secret Pals" for the year and have a great time doing secret things for their special person (and having special things done for them, too). We have a luncheon on the last day of school and disclose our Secret Pals with a short speech and a fun gift. *(Traverse Heights Elementary School, Traverse City, MI)*

How It Works: At the beginning of the year, those who are interested in participating fill out a "Secret Pal Data Sheet." They then draw names of other participants. Identities are not revealed until the end of the year.

Throughout the year, Secret Pals do nice things for the person whose name they drew, e.g., give a small gift or do something special for birthdays, anniversaries (marriage and/or employment), and holidays; send poems, notes of encouragement, or recordings of upbeat songs, etc.

At the end of the year, Secret Pal identities are revealed at a culminating event such as a picnic or luncheon. It's amazing how much participants learn about their fellow colleagues through this activity and how close Secret Pals become. *(Bonnie Walter, Lawrence, MI)*

Shhh . . . Don't tell who your Secret Pal is.

Secret Pal Data Sheet

Name _____

Home address _____

Birthday _____ Wedding anniversary _____

Employment anniversary _____ Home décor _____

Hobbies _____ Music preference _____

Books I like to read _____ Things I collect _____

Favorite food _____ Jewelry preference Gold _____ Silver _____

Other things I would like my *Secret Pal* to know about me _____

_____

Mascot

Universities have mascots such as Longhorns, Spartans, and Lions to symbolize their team spirit. Individual departments can communicate their spirit with a mascot as well. Once the group selects a symbol that best represents them, stuffed animals or pins can be made for each of the employees. Stickers can be made to put on certificates and memos, and mascot notecards can be printed. Logo pins can be used to represent the highest awards that can be achieved. Having a common mascot is fun and builds team unity.

GET-ACQUAINTED ACTIVITIES

Often we don't know or visit staff members who work in other departments or sections of the building. Create opportunities to get to know and learn more about each other and the organization in which you work.

One company tells of a vice president who had never been in the front lobby of the building where she worked for many years. She had a parking place in a secured area and always entered the building from the parking structure. One day there was a fire in the building and she had to enter through the front lobby. Although it was undamaged by the fire, she found the lobby to be less than attractive for conveying positive first impressions. The lobby was immediately remodeled. Sometimes we need an activity to take us out of our regular routines and give us a chance to learn about other areas and people in our workplace.

Looking Forward to Monday Morning

Bag-o-Folio

Prior to a meeting, send a notice to staff members asking them to bring three items in a bag that represent them. Some examples are:

- Running shoe—*I ran the NY Marathon.*
- High heel shoe—*I love to dance.*
- Plane ticket—*I love to travel.*
- Picture of family—*Family times are the best times.*
- Cooking spoon—*I love to cook.*
- Novel—*I relax by reading.*
- Miniature sewing machine—*Sewing is my hobby.*
- Diploma—*I just finished a Master's degree program.*
- Theater ticket—*In a theater is where I like to be most.*
- Picture of pets—*Animals are important to me.*

It's fun to see what type of bag the participants choose to hold their items. Some selected a bag from a favorite store because they love to shop there, others a bag that had dog pictures on it, some brought a travel bag because they love to travel, etc. (I was doing this activity in a hotel in Rhode Island and the manager asked me why all the participants had brought their lunches when lunch was going to be served. He thought the brown bags were filled with food!)

The day of the meeting, break the large group into small groups. Have each person share the contents of his or her bag with the other members of the group. Have the group select one person to be the spokesperson to the large group. That person can either share the items in his or her bag or select one item from each person's bag to tell about. It's amazing what commonalities are found among the people in the room and how people find others that they want to talk with at the break.

Bag-o-Folio

In a bag, bring three things that represent the kind of person you are (e.g., interests, hobbies, achievements). These will be shared with others.

A Week of Friendship

Do this activity on an individual basis and at the time of your choice. Don't do it for the entire staff or the integrity is lost.

Monday—

Smile at the people you see at work and give three of them genuine compliments.

Tuesday—

Express encouragement to someone you're friends with.

Wednesday—

Look for someone who needs a friend (a new staff person, someone who lives alone, etc.) and ask if he or she would like to have a cup of coffee or lunch with you.

Thursday—

Practice your listening skills. Select people you don't know very well and talk with him or her. Let the other person do the majority of the talking while you listen.

Friday—

Write a note or send a card to someone.

Saturday—

Think about your week, how you felt, how people you interacted with felt, and how you would like to spend next week. Do you want to turn some of these practices into habits?

In-House Open House

When my staff and I formed our new department, we held an "In-House Open House" and invited staff members to come to our new offices. We served refreshments and gave tours of our facilities. This event led to each department hosting an "open house" sometime during the year so that we all gained a better understanding of the role each department had in the organization. Some conducted tours, others showed a videotape, etc.

One group gave visitors a sheet of paper containing rhymes and room numbers. When the visitors went to the areas listed on the sheet, staff members gave them raffle tickets and signed the visitors' sheets. After all areas had been visited and signatures secured, everyone met in the cafeteria for refreshments and turned in the raffle tickets. A drawing was held to select prize winners.

Sample Special Ed. Facility Tour

In-House Open House

Name: _____

To learn about our program
And to have a little fun,
Take this to the office and
Turn in your check sheet when you're done.

At this time, your tickets
Will be taken from you, too,
And entered in the raffle.
We wish good luck to you!

Room 105
Once you've been to our room
And progressed to level three,
A privilege you'll have earned
Is to walk the hallways free.

Room 106
Stop in our room
And get your sheet.
We'll give you the points
For taking your seat.

Detention
You'll find in this room
The booth comes in twos.
Leave on your socks
But take off your shoes.

Room 101
Direct instruction.
How many groups are done?
Check it out
In Room 101.

Room 103
Only four
But sweet as can be.
Come watch our video
And you will see.

Room 104
Although our room
Is last in the hall,
We get backup
With a single call.

Miss Martin
When things aren't right
And you're feeling uptight,
Who you gonna call?
The lady down the hall.

Miss Swanson
Mainstream, medications,
Clinic and locals, too.
We think we should clone her.
How about you?

*Thank You
For
Visiting Us!*

"Getting to Know You" Scavenger Hunt

At a group event, give staff members a scavenger hunt form such as this one and instruct them to find a person in the room who matches each of the statements on the form. Allow time to mingle and talk. You can modify the

Scavenger Hunt

Fill in the following by using a name no more than twice.
Completing item Number 19 is a must. **Find someone who . . .**

1. Was born outside of the U.S. _____
2. Can say "Good Morning" in another language. _____
3. Is wearing contact lenses. _____
4. Is in graduate school. _____
5. Drives a sports car. _____
6. Will be planning to take a trip this year. _____
7. Has an unusual hobby. _____
8. Is an only child. _____
9. Is very active in the community. _____
10. Plays a lot of tennis. _____
11. Has five or more children. _____
12. Works a second job. _____
13. Is taking dance lessons. _____
14. Is single. _____
15. Voted in the last presidential election. _____
16. Has been to Europe. _____
17. Has been to the Indianapolis 500. _____
18. Had another career before their current career. _____
19. You would like to get to know better. _____

sheet so it contains items that relate to your school or geographic area.

When it appears that all have completed their forms, ask them to sit back down. Go through each of the questions and ask people to identify who fits into each category, for example, *Who is an only child?* Staff members then tell whose name they had written on their sheets.

Variation: Prior to the meeting, have staff members write down a personal fact not commonly known or an anecdote about themselves and return it. Summarize each fact or story, put them all on one page, and distribute the sheet to all staff members. Include a list of staff members' names. Whether it is learning that a coworker was a belly dancer in college or that your boss has a pilot's license, the whole staff increases their knowledge and appreciation of their colleagues.

Interesting Facts	My Guess	Staff Names
Attended Outward Bound	_____	Susie Smith
Worked as a DJ in college	_____	Maggie Martin
Lived in Turkey for three years	_____	Tim Tiland
Met spouse on the Internet	_____	Patti Kaye
Has twelve grandchildren	_____	Michael Brown
Ran the Boston Marathon	_____	Juanita Ledezma
Does magic tricks	_____	Tom Nedrehoaff

Pass the Roll

Have several rolls of toilet paper available for this activity—the firmer the better. Pass the rolls around the room and ask the staff members to *take some.* While you're giving the instructions, wrap the toilet paper around your hand, showing that you're taking quite a bit of paper. After each staff member has taken his or her amount off the roll, that person passes it on to the next staff member.

Some is the operative word here. Ask the group to hold up their streamers. Usually there's at least one person who tore off only one square. When you identify that person, give him or her your long streamer of many squares. This will generate a lot of laughs.

Now ask the staff members to write one positive thing about themselves on each of the squares (e.g., *I'm a good cook, I love to laugh, I'm patient with my children, I have a great smile, etc.*). When they're finished documenting their strengths, have them break into small groups and share their lists with other staff members or, if time allows, have each person read his or her list to the whole group. Have staff members keep this list as a reminder to read on days when they don't feel worthwhile.

Variation: Have the staff pair up. The person whose birthday comes first in the year is Person #1 and the other is Person #2. Person #1 finishes the sentence starter, ***What I like about me is*** . . . with items that were written on the toilet paper or with new ones, for example,

What I like about me is that I'm a good cook.
What I like about me is that I'm loyal to my friends.
What I like about me is that I'm always on time.
What I like about me is that if I say I'll do
    something, I do it.

Person #2 listens to the list of sentences, and when Person #1 is through, says, *Isn't that wonderful!*

Person #1 and Person #2 then reverse roles. Person #2 recites the list and Person #1 listens and then says, *Isn't that wonderful!*

Person #1 now finishes the sentence, *What I like about you is . . .* with multiple responses, for example,

> *What I like about you is that you always have a smile on your face.*
> *What I like about you is that you never talk badly about your coworkers.*
> *What I like about you is that you wear such tasteful clothes.*
> *What I like about you is that you're willing to help others.*
> *What I like about you is how you love your grandchildren.*

Person #2 listens again, but this time the response is, *You sure know quality when you see it.* Then, just as before, the two people reverse roles. This activity usually generates a lot of laughter.

Hosted Staff Meetings

To facilitate staff members' knowledge about one another, hold each staff meeting in a different department or class-room. The person hosting the group begins the meeting with an overview of him- or herself: interests, background, family, etc. Having the staff develop their own Portfolios and sharing them with the group makes this activity very easy. It's interesting to find out how much we don't know about our colleagues and how much we have in common.

Who's Your Match?

Purchase inexpensive items in duplicate (e.g., two noise-makers, two Hawaiian leis, two yo-yos, two Pez candy dispensers, two slinkies, etc.). Put all items into a large bag or box. Each person reaches into the bag and chooses an item. When all participants have made their selections, they each have to find the person in the room who has the matching item. The

two people then become a team for events that require two people. If your team needs to have more than two people, have multiples of the same item in the bag, e.g., six yo-yos for a team of six people.

Samsung, a semiconductor company in Austin, Texas, welcomed over 140 visiting Korean Samsung workers for a summer. Each was partnered with an Austin employee who "adopted" him or her. At a wild and wacky ice cream social, visiting Koreans met their Texas partners through a matching game involving toys, noisemakers, and Hawaiian leis.

Balloon Foolery

Give each person a deflated balloon and a small piece of paper. Have them put their name on the paper and insert it into the balloons. Everyone blows up their balloon, ties it, and releases it in the room. Staff members retrieve a balloon, pop it, take out the piece of paper, and find the person whose name they have. Allow time for everyone to get acquainted.

Whistle Up a Group

Write the names of songs on pieces of paper according to the number of people you want in a group (e.g., three or four). Examples of songs you could use are:

Jingle Bells
Whistle While You Work
Row, Row, Row Your Boat
We're Off to See the Wizard
Here Comes the Bride
Pop Goes the Weasel
Happy Birthday
Take Me Out to the Ball Game

Give each person a piece of paper with the name of a song on it. Instruct everyone to whistle the song that appears on their paper and find others who are whistling the same song. For those who can't whistle, have them hum the tune instead.

When the group members have found each other, have each group whistle their song to the others so they can guess the title of the song.

I'm Only Half Without You

Give each person a name tag with half a name written on it, e.g., one tag has "Mickey" and the other has "Mouse." Have the staff members mingle until they find their partner. Other examples of names that can be used are:

Humpty Dumpty	Robin Hood
Santa Claus	Donald Duck
Snow White	Darth Vader
Little John	Maid Marian
Roy Rogers	Luke Skywalker
James Bond	Ally McBeal
Bing Crosby	Bill Cosby
Elton John	Lone Ranger

STAFF MEETINGS

Staff meetings are a necessary function of organizations. Although they often elicit grunts and groans, they're a means of opening up the organization and fostering communication. Making them fun events helps.

Feed Them and They Will Come

Having snacks and refreshments available increases the motivation for staff members to willingly attend meetings, especially at the beginning or the end of the day.

Theme Staff Meetings

Assign a theme to the staff meetings for the year. At each meeting have one person contribute something that represents the chosen theme, for example,

- Share their Professional Portfolio or information about what they like to do, their background, family, education, etc.
- Share a talent (music, juggling, story, poem, etc.).
- Share a story about an embarrassing moment.
- Give an overview of what they do at their job.

Goal-Setting Teams

It's easier to achieve a goal when there is encouragement. Ask staff members to set a personal or professional goal they would like to achieve during a designated time period. Examples could include: *I want to . . . lose ten pounds, learn how to use a software package, organize my photo albums, etc.*

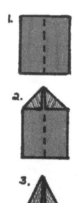

At a group event such as a staff meeting, have each person complete a goal sheet. Explain that the goal they write down will be shared with at least one other person, so they shouldn't write deep secrets. The paper should be at least 8 1/2" x 11" in size.

Have people make paper airplanes out of their goal sheets. In case someone doesn't know how to fold paper into an airplane, provide a diagram. It could be put on a transparency for the group to view or duplicated on the reverse side of the goal sheet.

When the airplanes have been assembled, have the staff members fly their planes across the room. Each person retrieves an airplane and becomes the support person to assist the owner of the airplane in reaching his or her goal.

Follow-up: If you set a time line such as one month, six months, etc., have the teams report to the whole group at the end of the time period. Describe what the goal was and

how it was achieved, e.g., *Maggie wanted to lose ten lbs., and we are happy to report that she exceeded her goal and has lost twenty-two pounds through diet and walking two miles a day.* You could also give reports along the way on progress made toward meeting the goal.

My Goal

(This will be shared with other people.)

Name _____

Phone _____ E-mail _____

Department _____

The goal I have set for myself is _____

_____

_____

_____

My time line is _____

You can help me reach my goal by _____

_____

_____

Five Minutes of Fun

Make a calendar of staff meetings. Ask "volunteers" to sign up for a meeting in which they will take responsibility for starting off the meeting with something fun. It could be a song, joke, story, reading, or an activity such as the one below. The activities need to be in good taste, though, so they won't offend.

5-Minute Quiz

Instructions:

Write the numbers 1–10 in a column. Beside #1, write down any number you want. Beside #2 and #6, write down the names of members of the opposite sex. Write anyone's name (e.g., friends or family) in the #3, #4, and #5 spots. Write down 4 song titles next to #s 7–10.

Key:

1. You must tell (the # in space 1) people about this game.
2. The person in space #2 is the one you love.
3. The person in space #6 is the one you like but can't work it out.
4. You care most about the person you put in #3.
5. The person you named in #4 is the one who knows you very well.
6. The person you named in #5 is your lucky star.
7. The song in #7 is the song that matches the person in #2.
8. The title in #8 is the song for the person in #6.
9. #9 is the song that tells you most about your mind.
10. And #10 is the song telling how you feel about life.

Appreciation Sound Off

Start staff meetings with a time to *Sound Off* about the things that have gone well since the last meeting.

Looking Forward to Monday Morning

Circle Massage

Before you get into the "business" of the staff meeting, ask people to stand up and form a single-file line or circle. Tell them to place their hands on the shoulders of the person in front of them and give them a nice shoulder and neck massage. First, have them pretend they're making a pizza and kneading the dough. Then have them switch to making karate chop movements on the back, and end with light "raindrops." After a few minutes, have the group reverse directions and give a massage to the person who is now in front of them. Oh, it feels so good to have some of the tension released!

"Splitting the Take"

Start your meetings with a 50/50 drawing in which people can buy a raffle ticket for $1. A duplicate-numbered ticket is put into a container. A ticket is drawn from the container and the matching ticket holder gets half of the money collected. The other half can go for a mutually agreed upon activity, e.g., purchasing items for the break room, a donation to a charity, student scholarships, etc.

Staff Raffle

Hold a raffle at staff meetings. Raffled items might be a sample that a salesperson has dropped off, a gift from a business partner, or a gift certificate for a gourmet delight made by the boss! *(Traverse Heights Elementary School, Traverse City, MI)*

Kazoo to You

I spent 30 years in Kalamazoo, Michigan, known as *K'zoo*, where kazoos were fun musical instruments. Give staff members kazoos, and when something is said that they agree with or like, instead of clapping have them blow their kazoos.

Word Bingo

Make a sheet like the one below that lists words, acronyms, phrases, etc., that are commonly used in your organization. Give each staff member a copy of the sheet and explain that to win, they simply need to mark off five squares in one staff meeting. They then shout, *Bingo!,* and receive a prize. If there is no winner, distribute new game sheets at the next meeting. You'll be amazed at how the staff's listening skills will be enhanced.

Staff Meeting Bingo

Instructions: Simply mark off five squares during one meeting and shout, BINGO! *It's that easy!*

Paradigm Shift	Rigorous Curriculum	Long-Range Plans	At the End of the Day	Time on Task
Revisit	Professional Development	Best Practice	Authentic Assessment	Under the Gun
Lesson Plans	Touch Base	Portfolio	Student Achievement	State Goals
Go the Extra Mile	Benchmark	The Big Picture	Cost Effective	School Improvement
Ballpark	Proactive, Not Reactive	Mind-set	Think Outside of the Box	Walk the Talk
Results-Driven	Empower Students	Fast Track	Stretch the Envelope	Knowledge Base
Site-Based	Outcomes	Student Driven	Parent-Teacher Conferences	Spring Break

Looking Forward to Monday Morning

Chapter 5
Through the Day

PROFESSIONAL DEVELOPMENT FUN

Pop-Ins

Have "Pop-Ins" on Friday afternoon. The administration provides pop and popcorn while the staff previews new videos and/or instructional materials they may be considering. It's also a time to discuss how everyone feels about the business at hand. This activity provides an opportunity for bonding and sharing. It is totally voluntary, but yields a high percentage of participants.

Brown Bag Book Discussions

Select a mutually agreed upon book related to your organization, to leadership, etc. The group meets on scheduled days to discuss the book while they are having lunch.

Lunch and Learn

Schedule informational topics to be presented while staff members eat lunch. The topics don't have to be occupationally related; they can also be on health, personal finance, retirement, etc. Lake Forest Hospital in Lake Forest, Illinois, has this lead on their notices: "Grab some lunch and then come in and feed your brain as well as your body."

FOOD & FUN

Drive your staff happy with these fun activities:

Food Festival

Each department selects a country and prepares food dishes representative of its culture. Tables are set up with the flag of each nation represented and authentic decorations. Each table has an assortment of ethnic foods, and staff members visit the various departments and have gourmet delights throughout the day. *(Linda Garcia, Kalamazoo, MI)*

Bagel Monday

Meet the staff at the door on Monday morning wearing a "Looking Forward to Monday Morning" T-shirt and a smile and holding a tray of bagels. Greet them by saying, *It's good to see you. It's going to be a good Monday.* Be a model for contagious enthusiasm. (Don't look at your watch if they arrive to work late!) *(See the form at the back of this book to order T-shirts.)*

Looking Forward to Monday Morning

Popsicle Day/Hot Chocolate Day

Give staff members a Popsicle on a hot day to help to cool down the temperature! In the winter, serve hot chocolate—don't forget the mini-marshmallows!

"Mondays Are a Special Grind"

Mondays Are a Special Grind

Make a sign saying, **Mondays Are a Special Grind,** and put it above the coffeepot. Instead of having the usual coffee, have gourmet coffee brewing for the staff.

Sundae Monday

Provide all the fixings for ice cream sundaes and allow the staff to create their own scrumptious delights.

M & M's = Monday Mornings

Greet the staff at the door on Monday morning with M & M candy—"Monday Morning" treats! *(Manufactured by Mars, Inc.)*

Take the "Ouch" Out of Monday

Greet the staff at the door with a "Choc-Aid"—a chocolate candy molded in the shape of a bandage. *(Manufactured by Lemberger Candy Corp., Paramus, NJ)*

"LUNCH BUNCH" ACTIVITIES

Lunchtime lends itself to socialization, and typically you choose a group of people (your "lunch bunch") to eat with. Make your Monday lunches exciting by trying some of the following ideas.

Monday Brown Bag Lunch Exchange

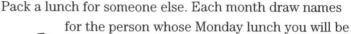

Pack a lunch for someone else. Each month draw names for the person whose Monday lunch you will be preparing. You may or may not want to keep the names anonymous. Drawing a specific person's name allows you to create "gourmet delights" you know that person likes, e.g., brownies, fruit, etc.

OR

Have everyone bring in a lunch, put them all in a common place, and have each person select a lunch from the bunch. Decorating the bag or making some other creative addition adds to the fun.

Theme Lunch Mondays

People often have specialties they love to create, e.g., breads, appetizers, salads, desserts, and so forth. Make a calendar for the year and designate the Monday after payday as a "theme lunch." People can sign up for the day they would like to bring in something to share. Theme days could include:

- Ethnic foods
- Crockpot cuisine
- Salads
- Creative sandwiches
- Appetizers
- Desserts
- Soups
- Chef's choice.

Each participant should provide copies of the recipes for others that could be compiled into a staff cookbook.

Group Lunch

Order pizzas or party-size submarine sandwiches to be delivered and divide the cost.

Looking Forward to Monday Morning

Chili Potluck Mondays

On a designated Monday, have all participants bring in their favorite version of chili. If you have a large staff, have different groups of people bring a chili contribution each Monday for a month. Have sour cream, shredded cheddar cheese, and hot sauce available as condiments. Make sure the recipes are duplicated for everyone. You could compile them into your own chili cookbook and share it with other staff members.

Here's a good one:

White Chicken Chili

Ingredients:	2 cups flour
	1 stick butter
	1 large onion
	2 stalks celery
	1/2 cup green chilies
	1/2 cup jalapeño peppers
	3 tablespoons cumin
	1/2 gallon chicken stock
	1 whole chicken, cooked and diced
	3 cans great northern beans
	Sour cream
	Shredded cheddar cheese
Process:	Chop and sauté onion and celery in the butter until translucent. Add flour and mix well. Turn up the heat and add remaining ingredients except the sour cream and cheese. Bring to a boil for one minute.
Serve:	Top with sour cream and finely shredded cheddar cheese.
Yield:	1 gallon *(Bill Warren, South Haven, MI)*

National Celebrations Calendar

National Soup Month is only one of many weeks or months designated by food manufacturers to feature and advertise a food product. It would be fun to follow the calendar for the year and plan a Monday lunch to coincide with these food themes.

January—
Hot Tea Month
Oatmeal Month
Soup Month
Prune Breakfast Month *(I'll pass on this one.)*

February—
National Snack Food Month
Potato Lovers' Month

March—
National Noodle Month
American Chocolate Week (fourth week in March)

April—
Egg Salad Week (the week after Easter—makes sense!)

May—
National Barbecue Month
National Egg Month
National Salad Month

June—
Dairy Month
National Fresh Fruit and Vegetable Month
National Iced Tea Month

July—
Baked Bean Month
Hot Dog Month
Ice Cream Month

September—
National Chicken Month
National Rice Month
National Honey Month

Looking Forward to Monday Morning

October—
> Pasta Month
> Pizza Month
> Seafood Month

November—
> Peanut Butter Lovers' Month
> Split Pea Soup Week (week of the second Monday)

Pop Can/Vending Machine-Funded Lunches

Often the time allocated for lunch makes it difficult to go out for a meal and be back to work on time. When there is a bottle or can deposit required for beverage containers, the proceeds for those returns are sometimes collected or the profits from the break room vending machines are used to fund staff lunches. Some events could be Soup and Grilled Cheese Sandwich Day, Pizza and Salad Day, etc. *(Linda Garcia, Kalamazoo, MI)*

Leftovers Potluck

After holidays, or when you host weekend events, the refrigerator is usually bulging with leftovers. Bring them in to share with other staff members for lunch.

Salad Bar Potluck

Everyone signs up to bring in an item for a Salad Bar Lunch. The sign-up helps to ensure that there will be a variety of items—not just carrots!

Outdoor Barbecues

Employees wanting to take a break from their regular lunch routine can enjoy an on-site outdoor barbecue. Burgers, bratwurst, grilled chicken, corn on the cob, and potato salad are items that the cafeteria might feature during summertime outdoor barbecues. *(Abbott Laboratories, Abbott Park, IL)*

Cafeteria Lunch Contest

Have a contest for people to submit their entries on the topic, "Why I like cafeteria lunch." If this is implemented in a school, divide the competitors into grade levels such as K–3, 4–5, and Adults (teachers, administrators, etc.). The entries could be expressed in the form of poems, songs, raps, and essays . . . any medium of creativity.

The winners receive free cafeteria lunches for a specified period of time and have their entries published or read to the school. This event could coincide with School Lunch Week (the second week in October) or be held at any time of the year. *(Paw Paw Public Schools, Paw Paw, MI)*

Shimmy, Shimmy Lunch

*(To the rhythm and rhyme from the movie **Big**.)*

The lunch goes down, down,
Baby, down, down to the trays.
Sweet, sweet burgers,
Better ones you'll never know.
Shimmy, shimmy tater tots. Shimmy, shimmy pop.
Shimmy, shimmy tater tots. Shimmy, shimmy pop.
I ate a beef stew with biscuits.
I said biscuits, not Triscuits.
Ice cream shakes, a cherry on the top,
Ooohh, the taste, the taste you cannot beat, 5 times a week.
I ate it, I drank it, I had to charge one credit.
It's cool, it's hot,
Fill my stomach 3 more times.

Marc Hodges—Grade 4
Paw Paw Public Schools, Paw Paw, MI

Lunchtime Laughs

During lunchtime show a funny video in the lounge or in a room not otherwise in use.

Empty Bowl Lunch

Staff members skip lunch and donate the cost of the lunch to a local soup kitchen. Those who can't go without lunch can also donate the price of the lunch to this cause. *(Birmingham Public Schools, Birmingham, MI)*

Lunchtime Field Trips

Although we worked in the state capital city, many of us had never been to the capitol building. Once a month we scheduled a field trip at lunch where we went together to visit various sites or attend events in the city. Often there are musical groups performing during the day in the summer. A walk in a quiet spot or a visit to a museum is fun.

Picnic in the Park

Things were getting really hectic at work, so I arranged a surprise outing. At lunchtime I told everyone to carpool and follow me. We went first to have neck massages and then to the park, where I had pizzas delivered. We talked, laughed, and relaxed. We all felt much better the second half of the day than we did during the first.

Out-to-Lunch Monday

If you and your coworkers typically go out to lunch on Fridays, change it to Monday. There are many good things happening on Fridays—payday, the start of the weekend. Make Monday the day you treat yourself. You could make it "date night" with your significant other, too.

Gourmet Pizza Mondays

One Monday a month, have gourmet pizzas delivered from a local restaurant or create your own. There are so many fun combinations that are available; you can try a new one each month.

YOUR ATTITUDE IS SHOWING!

It's easy to be trapped in negative attitudes. Our outlook on life is conditioned by our thoughts. If you allow yourself to indulge in gloomy, pessimistic thinking, it will show in the sour expression on your face. If you think happy, optimistic thoughts, your face will show happiness. Your attitude is your self-picture. Do a self-check to see if you light up the room when you walk into it—or out of it. Avoid negative, toxic people, especially in places such as the "Ain't It Awful Lounge." Chronic complainers are like poison to those striving to maintain positive attitudes. Speak highly of your coworkers and yourself.

You think 50,000 thoughts in a day, so keep them positive, especially on Monday.

Say No to "Moandays"

Designate every Monday as "Positive Day." Any person who is caught saying anything negative is assessed a fine. The money collected goes for a future fun activity. So . . . you can't complain about your team losing, rainy weekends, housecleaning, etc.

Restroom Readings

Often the only quiet we have in a workday is the few moments we spend in the restroom. Periodically in the past I've put positive sayings or cartoons on the wall (or they can be put in the stalls). Soon others were making their own contributions to "The Wall." At the end of the year, I had the messages duplicated and gave copies to staff members to keep.

Note: Be sure to tell the custodian you're doing this. When I put the first posting up, I noticed that the next day it had been removed. I thought, "Well, maybe someone has taken it down to duplicate it," so I put up another copy. The next day it was down again—and the day after that. Finally,

> *A bad attitude is like a flat tire. You can't go anywhere until it's changed.*

> *I have found that most people are about as happy as they make up their minds to be.*
> —Abraham Lincoln

I realized that the custodian was removing them in her efforts to keep the restrooms neat.

Word of the Week

Make a monthly calendar in which each week has a theme, e.g., Teamwork, Goals, Laughter, Risk Taking, etc. Select a staff person to read quotes related to the week's theme over the PA system each morning. Place the quotes in conspicuous places to reinforce the thought of the day, e.g., on the cash register at lunch, on the bathroom stall door, on bulletin boards, in daily memos, on badges, etc.

Word of the Week	Monday	Tuesday	Wednesday	Thursday	Friday
					1
Teamwork	**4** As you move ahead, help others move ahead with you. You will always stand tall with someone else on your shoulders. —*Bob Moran*	**5**	**6** T = Together E = Everyone A = Achieves M = More	**7** Teamwork is the ability to work together toward a common vision . . . It is the fuel that allows common people to attain uncommon results.	**8**
Goals	**11** When we set exciting, worthwhile goals for ourselves, they work in two ways: we work on them, and they work on us. —*Bonnie Pruden*	**12**	**13** Reach high, for the stars lie hidden in your soul. Dream deep, for every dream precedes the goal. —*Pamela Starr*	**14**	**15** No matter what you say or do to me, I am still a worthwhile person.
Laughter	**18** The most wasted day of all is that on which we have not laughed.	**19** If you can find humor in anything, you can survive it. —*Bill Cosby*	**20** Laughter is contagious. Start an epidemic.	**21** A sense of humor can help you overlook the unattractive, tolerate the unpleasant, cope with the unexpected, and smile through the unbearable.	**22**
Go For It! Risk	**25** People know you for what you've done, not for what you plan to do.	**26** No one is perfect. That's why pencils have erasers.	**27** Luck is a matter of preparation meeting opportunity. —*Oprah*	**28** A great pleasure in life is doing what people say you cannot do.	**29** You can't go through life without dings in your doors.

"... it's the instruction manual for your new computer."

Humor Bulletin Board

Designate a bulletin board where jokes can be posted. The rule is that anything posted must be tasteful (no ethnic, blonde, or religious jokes). Candid photos may be taken of staff members and posted.

Liven Up Communications

Jokes, anecdotes, and cartoons are great additions to memos, news-letters, and calendars. Again, make sure they're tasteful and non-offensive. *(See the order form at the back of this book to order **Laugh Lines**, a book of humor.)*

Laugh at Life

Children laugh 400 times a day—adults only four. Where does all the laughter go? I have a theory that it goes to your hips and gets stored there waiting to get out (but I can't prove it). Laughter is a sign of healthy self-esteem and adds to a positive attitude. Bill Cosby said, *If you can find humor in anything, you can survive it.* Mistakes become "learning experiences" when you can laugh at them. Find the humor in what you do throughout your life.

Ask staff members to share the most embarrassing or funny moments of their careers. You might put those stories in a booklet, periodically place them in the staff newsletter, or use them to begin a staff meeting. Younger employees who are just starting out are glad to see that everyone has had "experience-gaining moments" in their careers.

Sometimes things happen to us that are so devastating that we just can't talk about them. When we finally tell the story—give our demon a name—it's usually not as bad as we thought and we can finally laugh about it.

My friends created an award for the person who did the most embarrassing thing. Our award was a Wyler's Lemonade baseball cap, only because someone donated it. From then on it became known as *The Wyler's Award.* At the end of the year, on a group trip, or during a team project, everyone told stories about their most embarrassing moments. The group decided who was the most deserving of this prestigious award. I was the recipient on several occasions.

Who's Backward?

I was raised by an Army Colonel who was loving but very strict. In high school I was expected to be a prim and proper young lady. Despite my desire to wear a black dress to the formal and semi-formal school events, wearing black was considered "too mature" for my age.

When I went away to college, I bought my first black cocktail dress to wear to a fraternity homecoming dance. The dress had a high neck and no decoration of any kind in the front. The back, however, had a low V that was closed by a fabric crossover belt that wove through a large rectangular rhinestone buckle. I thought I was the most classy, sophisticated young woman at the party.

At about midnight, I noticed another girl on the dance floor who wore a black dress with the same type of rhinestone buckle that my dress had—only her buckle was in the front. I noticed that her dress also had a V, but it too was in the front, and she filled it with ease. We had on the identical dress—but one of us had it on backward. I raced to the restroom. It was ME! Aside from the manufacturer's tag being in front, I had darts on my back where the bust line was supposed to go, and slash pockets over my hips. I wanted to die of embarrassment. I told my date we had to go home—NOW! Hopefully no one but me noticed, but it was years before I could even speak of what had happened. Now I think it's hilarious.

Not So Appetizing

I went to dinner with a very good friend of mine. The restaurant was dimly lit, which added to the ambiance. We ordered liver paté as an appetizer. When it was served, it was resting on a solid block of something we couldn't identify. I took a small bite of the base, which tasted like margarine, and told my friend that I thought it was just a part of the presentation and not something that was to be eaten. He tasted it, loved it, and proceeded to eat the entire block. I asked the waiter what the substance under the paté was. He said it was chicken fat that the chef refrigerated to harden into a base on which to place the paté. My friend was in shock—not exactly a low-fat appetizer! He would have won *The Wyler's Award* for sure!

Name That Bride!

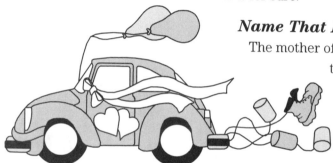

The mother of one of my friends was engaged. Both the prospective bride and groom were well into their eighties, and the wedding had to be moved up when the groom had signs of heart problems. At the wedding, my friend congratulated his mother on her marriage and asked what her new name was. "Hmmm . . ." she said. "I don't remember. I guess it wouldn't be very appropriate to ask my husband what it is, would it?"

NO SPECIAL REASON . . . JUST FOR FUN

I had a coworker who would frequently say, "If they wanted it to be fun, they would have called it 'fun,' but they call it 'work.'" Needless to say, he was not a joy to be around on the job. It's important to have fun at work often—not just on holidays. Lighten up! Think funny faster! At all costs, hold onto and cherish your sense of humor.

Talent (and Talentless) Show

The schools in one Texas school district are divided into five areas called "vertical teams." Each area team was asked to develop an act and, of course, the challenge was to outperform the other teams.

A Little Song, a Little Dance, a Little Seltzer Down the Pants . . .

Whatever your talent, stardom is waiting for you at the

Administrative Workshop Talent Show

— Monday, August 4 —

Entertainment provided by each Area

Call your Area Superintendent to join the show!

Do It Today!

Group Songs

One group wrote a song full of inside jokes and sang it to the tune of "Y.M.C.A."

M.I.S.D.
(initials of school district)

School's back.
It's here again.
We say, "Here goes,"
It's about to begin.
We know school's here,
Doesn't leave time to sin,
But we love our schools . . .
    (dun, dun, dun) (repeat)
. . . Cause we're committed to
M.I.S.D.
Let's hear it, everyone
M.I.S.D.
We will bring up the TAAS
Or we'll hear from the
    boss.
And we'll write CIPs
And work CACs.
Right here in
M.I.S.D.
Wish they paid us more in
M.I.S.D.
As you can clearly see,

We are Area 3,
And we are mighty fond
Of our Coach Maggie.
Now everybody sing,
M.I.S.D.
One more time, sing it:
M.I.S.D.
Wish the mail would stop.
Yes, it's piled to the top,
And the meetings don't cease.
Next July will be peace.
Yes, it's all about
M.I.S.D.
That's who we're loyal to
M.I.S.D.
Where you dial 414
When you can't take much more.
And the stress takes its toll,
But we lead it with soul.
Yes, we love our jobs.
    M.I.S.D.
    We hope we keep our jobs.
    M.I.S.D.
    This song is over now.
    M.I.S.D.
It's someone else's turn.
M.I.S.D.

Another group of counselors started their year with a song called, "The Counselor," sung to the tune of "The Wanderer." They dressed up with sunglasses and added dance steps to their folly.

The Counselor

(4 measure of 4; 1 count to 16)

Well, I'm the kind of girl
Who likes to have a ball,
I'm never in one place,
I roam from hall to hall.
And if you ask me just
How I spend my time,
I'll tell you 'bout this job of mine
    that is so divine . . .

Well, I'm the counselor,
They call me the counselor.
I roam from hall to hall to hall to hall.

Well, there're teachers on my left,
And there're parents on my right.
I have a family sitting at home
That won't get dinner tonight!
But if you ask me what part
Of my job that I detest,
Well, I'll open up my door
And show you those papers on my desk . . .

'Cause I'm the counselor,
They call me the counselor.
I roam from hall to hall to hall to hall to hall.

Well, we work hard every day.
We go through life with average pay.
But we're happy as can be,
Seems like a million kids have signed
    up to see me!

Well, I'm the type of gal,
Who'll never settle down.

If a kid needs a friend
I hope that I'm around.
I kiss 'em and I hug 'em
And I tell 'em they're great,
Then I rush 'em off to class
And say, "Now, hurry, don't be late."

'Cause I'm the counselor,
They call me the counselor.
I roam from hall to hall to hall to hall to hall.

— *Musical Bridge* —

(12 measures of 4; count to 4 twelve times)

Well, we work from sun to sun,
Our job is never done.
I wouldn't trade a thing,
It's the joy that my job brings.
And if you want to know more
About who I do this for,
Just walk right into my school,
And see those kids that I adore.

'Cause I'm the counselor,
They call me the counselor.
I roam from hall to hall to hall to hall to hall.

Yes, I'm the counselor,
I'm glad I'm the counselor.
I answer calls and calls and calls and calls
    and calls.

'Cause I'm the counselor,
They call me the counselor.
I roam from hall to hall to hall to hall to hall.

Yes, I'm the counselor,
I'm glad I'm the counselor.
I answer calls and calls and calls and calls
    and calls.

"Fashion (T)hat!"

"We wear many hats in our jobs" was another group's theme. They had a hat fashion show highlighting the many hats they wear while performing their jobs. Staff members came out individually wearing a particular hat, while the narrator told about it and what it represented. Some examples are:

Cowboy Hat	We're quick on the draw with our cell phones. (Model pulled a cell phone out of a holster.)
Nurse Cap	We're always helping the sick students to get well.
Sailor Cap	We're accustomed to dealing with the language we hear in the halls.
Halo	Because we pray for guidance.
Mortar Board	For the knowledge we must have in many areas.
Hard Hat	To wear during the construction and renovation projects that are always going on in the schools.
Visor	To demonstrate our "financial expert" skills with school budgets.
Beret	To demonstrate our design skills in creating a warm, friendly place.
Football Helmet	To use with our strong negotiation skills.
Sherlock Holmes Hat & Magnifying Glass	For all the investigations we do to get to the bottom of things.
Social Hat	Because we're so glad to be here. (The model turned away from the audience and there was a pair of lips attached to her hips!)

Let your imagination run wild to come up with other hats that you wear while doing your job.

Looking Forward to Monday Morning

The Great Coffee Mug Adventure

A friend of mine "borrowed" a colleague's favorite coffee mug and the adventure began. The coffee mug accompanied numerous people as they traveled. At each destination a picture was taken of the mug (the cup—not the face of the traveler) in the appropriate surroundings. For example, at Disney World a picture was taken of Mickey Mouse holding the mug. A note was attached saying what a good time the mug was having in the sun and how nice Mickey and Minnie had been to it. The note was signed, "Miss you, Your coffee mug." When the pictures continued to come in over a period of several years, a scrapbook was made of all the adventures it had had. When its owner retired, the mug was returned.

This picture was taken at a conference that the mug's owner wasn't able to attend.

Riddle Contest

Make up riddles about staff members. Put them in the staff newsletter and have people guess who they think the riddle is describing. Have staff members submit their votes and hold a drawing from the correct answers collected. The winner receives a token prize. Be sure to publish the answers.

"Clean It Up!" Day

I have always felt guilty if I took work time to sort files, dust shelves, etc., in my office because it felt like I wasn't "working." However, I'm much more productive when there is order around me. Make cleaning up the office a fun event. Our staff designated the last hour of each Friday as cleaning time, when everyone straightend up their desks, counters, and so forth.

You can also have a cleaning "event" where you designate a certain day for all office staff to purge files, dust, etc. Nationally, January 10 is "Find the Top of Your Desk Day," so that would be an ideal time to schedule it. Make sure you have cleaning supplies and large trash containers available. Give prizes for such things as "The Most Improved Office," "The Greatest Number of Pounds of Stuff Thrown Away," and so forth. Post the winners' names in a public place and be sure to take pictures. *(Abbott Laboratories, Abbott Park, IL)*

"Why I Like Working at . . ."

Have a contest—with good prizes—for the staff to submit their creative entries to describe why they like working at _____(name of organization). The directions can be given in poetic fashion to set the tone.

Why I Like Working at . . .

Come one! Come all! Come everyone!
Stop what you're doing and join in the fun.
There's a time to work, but we need to play
To relieve the stress of a hard-fought day.

No one among us has no need to rest
So come along and give us your best.
The test is of talent for all who apply,
To be the best at "whatever" in the judge's eye.

Whether you sing or dance or poetry spout,
You're sure to have fun with our creative "out."
If music and song are your forte,
Come serenade us in a harmonious way.

Do you lean toward comedy for others' enjoyment?
Then share with us the joys of employment.
Whatever your talent, please bear in mind,
What pleasures of working here do you find?

Weave in the reasons you'd ne'er want to leave,
The ideas and thoughts as you so perceive.

Looking Forward to Monday Morning

Be it coworkers or paydays, activities, or hours,
Retirements, birthdays, or baby showers.

Whatever your reasons, it need not be long,
Just put it to music, to rhyme, or to song.
Finish one, two, or three, and delights you will see,
For prizes abound for the winners three.

So give it your all, give it your best,
Put your creative side to the test.
Use your talents, whatever they may be,
To bring joy and laughter to all who see.
(Bill Warren and Esther Wilkinson, South Haven, MI)

One woman's winning entry gives many reasons why
she likes her job. *(Barbara Coombs, Lawton, MI)*

The Top 10 Reasons I Like Working at M.I.S.D.

#10 Traveling far can be a pain,
But my distance to work is rather sane.

#9 Our staff has grown larger, more come
than have gone.
United we stand, so we'll always be
strong.

#8 At social events, we invite everyone.
At parties, Olympics, we always have
FUN!

#7 I have variety in my job every day.
The boss even listens to what I say.

#6 For me, keeping busy is important, I know.
Never a problem with my paper flow.

#5 Communication is something I choose.
Thanks so much for the "Paycheck News."

#4 Health, dental, vision, and sick days, too.
The benefits are a plus for you.

#3 Bonnie Walter shares an office with me.
She brightens each day; it's plain to see.

#2 When it comes to bosses, mine's
considerate and kind.
She's the very best; there's no doubt
in my mind.

#1 The friends I have made throughout
the years,
Are the greatest gift and cause for
CHEERS!

In summary, it's a great place to be.
That's why I like working at M.I.S.D.

"Just Because" Messages

Deliver singing telegrams, balloons, stars, treats, or hugs to designated staff members "just because."

Door Decorating Contest

Hold a "Decorate Your Door" contest with a designated theme.

- Safety
- Homecoming
- Think Spring!
- How I Spent My Vacation
- Family
- Hobbies
- Holidays
- Seasons

Select a panel of peer judges to choose the winner(s). The contest could be held monthly, quarterly . . . as long as there is active interest and participation.

Personalized Lounge Door

Decorate the lounge door to represent the staff. Each staff member makes something that represents him or her and puts the contribution on the door.

Miniature Golf Tournament

Turn your workplace into an indoor miniature golf course. Create five or more holes of various lengths that require participants to putt down the hallways, around cubicles, under desks, around the trashcan, and into the hole. Have in-house tournaments, and when you get really good, challenge a neighboring school to a match. This could become a yearly event with rival districts or become an annual tournament with schools in the county.

Looking Forward to Monday Morning

"Bring Your Parents to Work" Day

In Chicago, WGN Radio has a talk show called "The Kathy and Judy Show." In one of their discussions they talked about how parents don't really have an understanding of what their adult children do at their jobs. They talked about the "Take Your Child to Work" Day concept and suggested that there be a day when parents accompanied their adult sons and daughters to work. Well, Mayor Richard Daley declared a "Bring Your Parents to Work" Day for the city, and it was a huge success. For example, at Midway Airport in Chicago, Southwest Airlines had parents assisting their children with their jobs, and WGN Radio had parents in the control room. Why not borrow the idea and schedule a day when parents are invited to accompany the staff to work?

Yearbook Photos

Most school yearbooks contain formal staff pictures. Alongside the current photo, put staff members' high school graduation pictures or photos of them when they were kids.

"Guess Who?" Contest

Our school had staff members bring in their baby pictures. We then numbered each photo and posted them in a display case. The students filled out ballots guessing which teacher was which baby. The following year, elementary school pictures were used. The kids and staff had great fun, and the children realized that the teachers were just like them. *(Traverse Heights Elementary School, Traverse City, MI)*

*"Jefferson" Hodges
Kalamazoo, MI*

Classic Car Show

Younger staff members drove their old cars to school, parked them on the grass, put up a "Classic Car Show" sign, and had a great time watching peoples' responses.

Car Show and Picnic

At the end of the year have a picnic/car show where staff members can display their car "treasures." People can bring in gorgeous restored vehicles, or those with a sense of humor can bring in vehicles such as a pop-up trailer or an inflatable car blown up and displayed with pride.

Pinewood Derby Race

Pinewood Derby races aren't just for Cub Scouts. They're great fun for everyone. Build your own derby from blocks of wood and have races. Kits can be purchased from hobby stores and creatively shaped and decorated.

Build Your Own Model Rocket

Purchase rocket kits at a hobby store and build your own model rocket. Hold a launching event. Prizes are optional, but lots of fun.

Misty Hodges

Pet or Mutt of the Month

Each month have staff members submit photographs of their dog/pet for display. Having pictures of the animals dressed in holiday costumes is really fun.

Staff Cookbook

While I was in Germany, I was given a cookbook titled, "Deliciously DoDDS (Department of Defense Dependents Schools)." It was a compilation of recipes from instructors who teach in the military schools in Europe and Asia.

This is an excellent project for a keyboarding class, a food services program, or a school fund-raising activity.

Looking Forward to Monday Morning

Consider compiling your own organization's cookbook, with staff members contributing their favorite recipes.

The recipe I always contribute is "All-Meat Stew."

All-Meat Stew

1 Elephant—medium size
2 Rabbits (optional)
Salt and Pepper

Cut elephant into small, bite-size pieces. Add enough water to cover. Salt and pepper to taste. Cook over kerosene fire for about 4 weeks at 465°. This will serve 3,800 people. If more are expected, 2 rabbits may be added, but do this only in an emergency as most people do not like hare in their stew.

Betting Pools

Form betting pools on events such as the Super Bowl, March Madness college play-offs, etc. These are legal as long as all of the money is distributed to the bettors.

Balloon Day

Greet the staff at the door and give each member a balloon.

CDs or Tapes

Purchase CDs or cassettes of music that have a purpose, e.g., relaxing, motivating, etc., and give them to staff members.

Skills Competition

Sponsor competitions to test each other's skills in activities such as hula hooping and bubble gum blowing.

Toilet Seat Challenge

Make a toilet seat or other unique item an award for departmental "challenges." The Toilet Seat Challenge begins with one group, e.g., administration, challenging another department in the activity of their choice. Challenges could be met shooting pool, playing chess, playing cards—anything that's fun. The losing group gets its name engraved on a brass plate that's affixed to the toilet seat. It's now their responsibility to challenge another group in the activity of their choice. *(Oswego High School, Oswego, IL)*

DRESS-UP EVENTS

"Think Summer!" Day

In the middle of winter have a "'Think Summer!' Day. Staff can wear Hawaiian clothes, shorts, etc. Serve lemonade and Popsicles as refreshments.

T-shirt or Sweatshirt Day

Everyone wears a sweatshirt supporting a favorite professional or college sports team. **Variation:** Everyone wears a shirt with a message on it (but only those in good taste). *(Birmingham Public Schools, Birmingham, MI)*

"Take Me Out to the Ball Game" Day

Opening day of baseball season is a symbol of spring and a reason (excuse) to celebrate. Invite staff members to wear the baseball paraphernalia, e.g., hats, buttons, T-shirts, logo socks, etc., of their favorite team.

Hat Day

The third Friday in January is designated as "Hat Day." During this day (or any day you want) staff members are encouraged to wear creative hats to work. Judging of the hats is optional. If judged, prizes are awarded for the most creative, the craziest, the most lovely, etc. *(Birmingham Public Schools, Birmingham, MI)*

Other Dress Day Ideas

Other types of dress days you could have are listed below. Joke prizes may be given if the events are judged.

- Fun/Ugly Tie Day
- Wild Socks Day
- Suspenders Day
- Cargo Pants Day
- Jeans Day
- Sports Team Uniform Day
- Crazy Eyeglasses Day

COUNTING THE DAYS

Counting off the remaining days until a special event in the future e.g., project completion, vacation, end of the year, etc., can be fun.

Countdown Chains

Cut construction paper into rectangular pieces equal to the number of days in the countdown. Write a number on each rectangle in large, bold print. Staple or glue the strips into chains with the numbers in reverse order. This activity may remind you of when you were a child and made chains to trim Christmas trees and classrooms. Drape the chain in a very visible area. Each day, remove a piece of the chain to reveal the number of days remaining until the event.

Tape Measure Countdown

To count down the last sixty days, hang a cloth tape measure in a visible place. As each day goes by, cut off an inch of the tape measure. The remaining inches indicate the number of days left until the designated date.

Toilet Paper Countdown

Count the number of days remaining until the event. Write numbers in reverse order on each square of toilet paper. When you've reached the final number, wind the squares back onto the roll. Make a large sign saying, "Days Remaining until _____" and hang the roll in an area where people congregate. Tear off a square each day to reveal the number of days remaining.

Days Remaining Until
Spring Break

Chapter 6
To the End & Beyond

"FUN-RAISERS" & COMMUNITY SERVICE

Dress Down for a Cause

As a fund-raiser for a worthy cause, staff members are allowed to dress down for a $3 donation to a designated charity. A badge is made for the participants to wear explaining the absence of the usual dress, while showing the organization's support for the cause. Posters may also be placed at the entrance of the building to inform the public about the fund-raising campaign. *(Birmingham Public Schools, Birmingham, MI)*

OR

At the beginning of the United Way Campaign, inform employees that those who turn in their pledges early are allowed to observe Casual Day dress practices for the balance of the week. For example, if the pledge is turned in on Monday, they have four days left to wear casual clothes that week. If the pledge is turned in on Tuesday, there are three days remaining for casual attire, etc. *(Aluminum Company of America, Pittsburgh, PA)*

The Power of Change

Identify causes that need financial assistance, e.g., a local resident who needs help to cover medical bills, a hospice, a domestic violence shelter, Habitat for Humanity, etc. Decorate receptacles such as birdhouses and place them near the vending machine and in the cafeteria lines and label them as the "Spare Change Fund." Each month identify a different charity and place information about the organization next to the collection receptacle. Post the total of each month's contributions for the staff to see and feel proud of.

In-House Bake Sales

To raise money for a cause or organization, have a series of bake sales where staff members bring in goodies to sell to their colleagues.

Back-to-School Packages

Starting a new school year is both exhilarating and terrifying for children. Having the proper school supplies and looking like the other kids in the class are important to their need to conform. Identify children in need of assistance and obtain their clothes and shoe sizes. Have the staff purchase and donate items (e.g., backpack, school supplies, jeans, shoes, etc.) to make the start of the school year a success for these children. *(Linda Gustafson, Milford, CT)*

LABEL IT GENEROUS

Businesses have been very generous in sponsoring partnership programs that allow schools to obtain computers or sports and audio-video equipment by collecting labels or other proofs of purchase. Ask the community-at-large to save designated food product labels or sales receipts that may be redeemed for the needed products. Make the collection of these labels an event.

No-Money Bake Sale

Hold a non-monetary bake sale where the items may only be purchased with a designated number of labels.

The Price of Admission

When you have a staff meeting, ask everyone to bring in a label for admission. Have them also "purchase" beverages and snacks with labels.

Charity Olympics

Communities often sponsor annual Charity Olympics in which employees from community organizations compete against each other to raise money for local charities. The competition is much different than the real Olympics in terms of events. For instance, one event might be to see how many balloons a team can stuff inside a T-shirt being worn by a team member. There is much less physical training needed for these contests!

You could develop your own Olympics and have various departments compete. Events should be fun—tricycle races, three-legged races, Frisbee toss, etc.

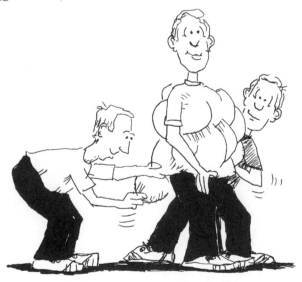

Participants attempt to stuff as many balloons as possible inside a T-shirt.

A Golden Tradition

I heard this tale before I moved to the Chicago area, and each year it was validated. How wonderful that there are people in the world who give to others without the expect-ation of being thanked or recognized.

An unknown person began dropping a one-ounce South African gold Krugerrand, worth about $300, into the Salvation Army collection kettle in front of a store. No one knows who the person is, and he or she continues to be anonymous, often hiding the coin in a piece of paper or in a bill. This is not a one-time occurrence. One year the Salvation Army collected thirty-four of these precious coins.

END-OF-THE-YEAR ACTIVITIES

Picture Your Year

Pat Bell
Austin, TX

Give each staff member a piece of newsprint and a magic marker and have them describe their year. Allow each

person time to share reflections . . . successes . . . learning experiences . . . adventures . . . laughs. If you have a large staff, divide the group into smaller groups. The year may be described in a picture, song, skit, etc.

Year in Review

Make a "Year in Review" booklet display-ing pictures and listing or describing achievements. Celebrate the journey of getting to where you are.

Staff Slide Show/Video

Capture the events of the year in a slide show or video. Show the production and reminisce during an annual celebration. It's sure to generate smiles and laughter.

Looking Forward to Monday Morning

Picture Challenge

Equipment needed: A Polaroid or digital camera for each group.

Divide the participants into equal groups. (Limit groups to a maximum of five or six members.) Having groups of unfamiliar participants promotes new friendships. Give each group a copy of the rules and read them to all the members.

RULES:

- You have exactly two hours to complete as many of the tasks as you can.
- You must have a picture of the group doing each of the tasks or with the items to share with the other groups.
- You will receive five points for each task you complete and have a picture taken by a group member.
- You will, however, receive ten points for every task you complete that has all group members present in the picture.
- You have no geographic boundaries.
- *Penalty:* There is a one-point penalty for every minute your group is late in returning to the starting site.

Take a picture of your group doing each of the following: (You will need to adjust these according to the time of year and your geographic location. This event took place in a rural area in October.)

1. 'Tis time for the Great Pumpkin to appear. Find a pumpkin and take your picture.
2. Have your group picture taken next to a statue.
3. Have your group picture taken with a non-domestic animal (no horses, cats, dogs, etc. I know, horses aren't domestic, but they don't count today).
4. Find a fire truck and/or car and pose as firefighters (police, sheriff, mail carrier, etc., are also acceptable.)
5. Pretend you're going to the Emerald City and find a scarecrow.
6. Have your picture taken next to something "sporty."

7. Up a creek without a paddle? Have your group picture taken in a canoe.

8. Have your picture taken near a pay phone.

9. Remember your childhood days? Have your picture taken with no fewer than three children.

10. Have your group picture taken in or by the fountain of your choice.

11. Gather all your members in a pickup truck for a Kodak moment and include the driver in your picture.

12. Up a tree? Have your picture taken with all members "up a tree."

13. Your choice. Bring a special picture back to share with the group.

Tally the total points and award a prize to the winning team. Display the pictures taken for all teams to see. Put the photographs in an album to review at the end of the year.

Golf Outing

Plan a golf outing in which all staff members—golfers and non-golfers—can participate. For instance, play a round in which you may hit with only two of your clubs. Or give each person a piece of string 36" long plus a pair of scissors. The players may move their balls out of the woods, sand traps, etc., but each time they do, they have to cut off a corresponding number of inches from their string. The winner is the person with the lowest score and the longest piece of string.

OTHER GROUP ACTIVITIES

Employee Chorus

Form an Employee Chorus to perform at various functions. *(Fulton County Schools, Atlanta, GA)*

Looking Forward to Monday Morning

Musical Group

Form a Jazz Band (or other musical group) to perform at work-related events. *(Fulton County Schools, Atlanta, GA)*

Flower Gardens

Divide the campus into areas and have teams design and plant flowers in their allocated area.

Vegetable Gardens

Plant a vegetable garden at work in which many staff members can participate. All staff members will have an opportunity to taste the fruits of their labors.

Culture Club

Bring together people who love the arts, and organize "outings" to concerts, museums, art exhibits, etc. Group discounts are often available to help defer costs. Bus trips to events in larger cities are also fun.

Corporate Olympics

Participate in the Corporate Olympics, which promotes community-wide interest in fitness, health, and wellness.

Even More Group Activities

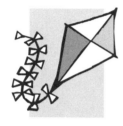

- Professional baseball games *(Fulton County Schools, Atlanta, GA)*
- Community festivals
- Bus trip to outlet shopping malls
- Group trip to amusement parks
- Volleyball games
- Walking or running group
- Aerobics
- Water aerobics
- Kite flying
- Cookouts after work
- Dance instruction, e.g., swing dancing, line dancing, etc.
- Softball leagues, departmental competition, or just-for-fun softball games
- Dart competitions
- Card game tournaments
- Three-on-three basketball tournaments
- Skiing
- Camping trips

Looking Forward to Monday Morning

AFTER-HOURS NETWORK

The networking that people do outside of the workplace assists in developing positive relationships on the job.

Bowling League

Form a non-sanctioned, handicapped bowling league where previous experience is not required for participation. Give a crash course on how to bowl and keep score for those who are new to the sport. Having FUN is the objective.

Bowl for a predetermined number of weeks, usually a semester, and end the season with a Fun Night. Give awards for such things as:

- Winning team
- High-scoring game, male and female, actual and handicapped
- Most improved bowler

Continue Fun Night with three games that follow a format such as:

GAME 1—Low Score Wins

A gutter ball on the first ball = STRIKE!
A gutter ball on the second ball = SPARE!

GAME 2—Crazy Frames Mix

1st Frame	Bowl with the opposite hand you normally use.
2nd Frame	Bowl normally.
3rd Frame	Bowl between your legs, facing backward.
4th Frame	Bowl normally.
5th Frame	Bowl on your knees.
6th Frame	Bowl normally.
7th Frame	Bowl by placing the ball on the floor and pushing it with your foot.
8th Frame	Bowl normally.

| 9th Frame | Sit down and push the ball with both feet. |
| 10th Frame | Bowl normally. |

GAME 3—No Tap

High score plus handicap wins.

Nine pins down on the first ball = STRIKE!

You don't have to bowl for the spare.

(Barbara Coombs, Lawton, MI)

Looking Forward to Monday Morning

Section III
Celebrating with Coworkers

All I wanna do is have some fun.
I got a feeling I'm not the only one.
—Sheryl Crow, Recording Artist

Chapter 7
Caring & Sharing

WELCOMING A NEW STAFF MEMBER OR BOSS

A certain amount of anxiety comes with any new job, whether the new person is a staff member or a boss. Feeling welcomed by the existing staff can help alleviate those "new job jitters."

Welcoming Activities

- Putting up welcome banners or electronic messages on a signboard.
- Holding a welcome gathering with cake and punch where the person has an opportunity to introduce and tell the group about himself or herself.
- Hosting a "Hi Tea" with tea and cookies where people can mingle.
- Giving the new person a welcome packet of items with the organization's logo, such as a pin, pen, sweatshirt, etc. Personalized items such as notepads and business cards are also effective.
- Including a short biography of each new staff member and a picture in the staff newsletter.
- Taking pictures of new staff members and displaying them in each department with a "Welcome" banner.
- Giving "A+" lapel pins for all new staff members to wear. *(Allegan Public Schools, Allegan, MI)*
- Giving a mug with the organization's mission statement printed on it.

New Staff Orientation

New staff orientation can be a time of high anxiety. In one of the school districts I worked for, we used cards that gave new people a chance to communicate what they were thinking and feeling, and to connect with others so they would feel more at ease in their new work environment. Before we got into the "business of the day," staff members completed the first two cards and then shared their responses with each other. At the end of the day, they were each given a third card with a school district pin attached to it.

On the way to work today I was thinking _____.

The thing I'm afraid of most about today is

_____.

The things I want to know by the end of the day are:

_____

_____

_____

_____

ADMINISTRATIVE PROFESSIONALS WEEK

Administrative Professional's Day, Secretary's Day, My-Right-Arm Day—whatever you call it, (the last full week of April) make it a Super Day! A study of professional secretaries revealed that as many as 30 percent would prefer a simple letter of appreciation from their managers, and that a bouquet of flowers or lunch was unnecessary. Only 7 percent of the respondents indicated that they had ever received such a letter.

In addition to a letter, other nice things you can do for the administrative assistant include:

- Taking turns answering the phones or performing some of their other duties.
- Bringing a special coffee or tea for his or her well-deserved break.
- If the assistant is female, giving her an assortment of bubble bath packets to use in the evening.
- Making a special certificate *(Lake Forest Hospital, Lake Forest, IL)* such as the following:

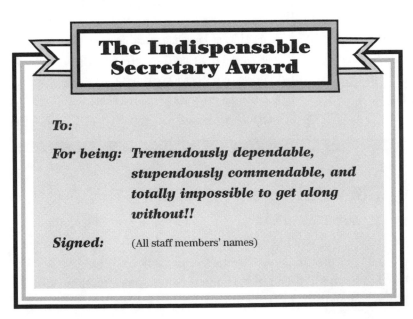

The Indispensable Secretary Award

To:

For being: *Tremendously dependable, stupendously commendable, and totally impossible to get along without!!*

Signed: (All staff members' names)

GET-WELL ACTIVITIES

When you're sick, you just don't feel good. It's times like these that a little TLC or thoughtfulness is appreciated.

Send a Poem

When I broke my elbow, I received this poem along with a teddy bear with its arm in a sling—just like me!

A Get-Well Poem

No somersaults, cartwheels, or handstands for you,
At least 'til you're healed, all mended anew.
You've got a boo-boo, your arm's in a sling,
The truth of it is, you've a broken wing.

It's a nuisance, a pain, inconvenient, too,
Especially for someone as active as you.
But follow the doc's instructions to a tee
And soon you'll be better. Believe me, you'll see!!!

I'm sorry you're hurting, but it won't be long,
You'll be back up to snuff with whistling and song.
If there's anything that you need me to do,
You know I'll be there to do it for you.

You'll be in my prayers. I'll think of you each day
To help speed your recovery in the most loving way.
Now take time to heal, it's an important task.
If there's anything you need, you know who to ask.

You'll need a companion while you're on the mend,
A cuddly, empathic, understanding friend.
He has a condition that's identical to yours,
It's the same length of time 'til he's on all fours.

So take him and hug him, make him your pal,
And remember, Diane, that you're quite a gal.
I wish you quick healing, complete and strong
And I'll send you a hug to speed it along.

(Bill Warren, South Haven, MI)

Gift-a-Day

My friend had breast cancer. After her surgery I gave her a basket of presents with instructions that she could open one gift per day. In it were items such as a book, book-on-tape, bubble bath, bath pillow, body cream, a pair of pillow cases, potpourri, stuffed bear, etc.

Get "Well"

Make a cardboard replica of a well with a crank and cord that goes into the container. Have staff members write cheerful notes to the person who is ill. Attach the notes to the cord and drop them into the well. As the ill person turns the crank, he or she can remove the notes and read the messages. *(John Speeter, Scotts, MI)*

Carpool Driver

The logistics of getting the kids to where they need to be can be a major ordeal. Take a turn at driving in the carpool.

"I/We Care" Kit

Make a kit of supplies specific to the illness. For example, for a cold the kit could include tea, honey, cough drops, lip balm, tissues, echinacea, etc.

Calculator Tape Messages

Have staff members write messages on a roll of calculator tape, roll it up, and take it to the person who is ill.

Humoring the Patient

Put Norman Cousins' philosophy of the healing power of laughter to the test by providing the patient with humorous cassettes or videotapes to laugh the hours away.

Meal Delivery

Even if the person who is sick doesn't have much of an appetite, the rest of the family does. Providing a meal allows the ill person to get some rest without worrying about whether other family members are eating.

Homemade Chicken Soup

This may be too obvious, but it really works.

BIRTHDAYS

Birthdays are a celebration of an individual and not a chronicle of years. Do NOT have "over the hill" parties and wear black armbands. Instead, celebrate the passages of life.

Honoree's Choice

The person who has the birthday brings in something to share with others, e.g., birthday cake, bagels, cinnamon rolls, etc. (I like this practice, as no one has to wonder if anyone will remember their birthday, and those who don't want their birthday acknowledged will get their wish.)

Birthday Cake Drawing

At the start of the year, have a "Birthday Cake Drawing." On the appropriate date, people provide a cake for the person whose name they drew. Find out what his or her favorite kind of cake is and bring it for all to share. Don't forget the forks, plates, and napkins.

Theme Birthdays

With a small staff, each birthday can be personalized and planned to correspond with the person's interests.

- If the person has a hobby such as collecting pig figurines, the theme for the birthday celebration could be, "It's Your Day, So Let's Pig Out." Everyone dresses in pink and wears elasticized pig noses. There are banners with pig pictures on them and all the gifts are pig-related. Everyone participates in chants—in Pig Latin, of course.

- "Lettuce Entertain You" is the theme for a vegetarian birthday celebration. People bring ingredients for a salad bar and dress as the fruit or vegetable of their choice—a peach of an idea. One of the more clever outfits I saw had a piece of paper with "6/12/03" on it. It took me a while to determine that the fruit it was depicting was a date—cute!

- For a wine lover, the theme could be "You are the Grapest." Make purple the color of the day and decorate with purple balloons. Have everyone dress in purple clothes. The refreshments could include sparkling grape juice and cheese, and the gifts might be all wine-related. Real wine can be given with personalized wine labels if appropriate.

- For the boss, the theme is "You're the Top Banana." Everyone wears yellow and the office is adorned with bananas. The refreshments feature banana splits or banana cream pies.

- Another theme idea for the boss' birthday could be "For the Big Cheese." You might serve an assortment of cheese, crackers, and fruit and give either "cheesy" (funny) gifts or "nice" gifts that relate to cheese.

Address Book

Obtain the employee's address book or e-mail directory. Send a notice to each person listed indicating that your coworker's birthday is coming up soon. Ask them to send a card, a note with a memory included, or some words of wisdom to the birthday person.

Affirmations

Give staff members a card on which they can write how their lives have been enhanced by knowing the person whose birthday is coming up. Put the cards in places where the birthday person will find them throughout the day.

It's the Season

Celebrate all staff members' birthdays for the year in the month of January. The first week of the month, celebrate the birthdays that fall in January, February, and March. Have refreshments that represent winter, such as hot chocolate and cake. The second week, celebrate the birthdays that fall in April, May, and June, and have a spring theme. The third week, celebrate the July, August, and September birthdays. You can serve summer refreshments such as lemonade, Popsicles, or ice cream cones. The last week, celebrate the birthdays of October, November, and December, for which cider and donuts are appropriate treats.

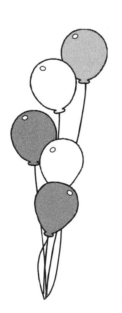

Balloon Bouquet

Present or have a balloon bouquet delivered to the birthday person with a special message attached.

Birthday Relief

On the staff person's birthday, have the principal relieve the teacher for a designated amount of time. The principal could conduct a special activity with the students while the teacher uses the free time to get caught up.

Looking Forward to Monday Morning

Marker Birthdays

When a person has a decade-advancing birthday (30, 40, 50, 60), give him or her the appropriate number (30, 40, 50, 60) of a single item, such as:

- Daffodil bulbs
- Golf balls
- Packets of flower seeds
- Balloons
- Suckers
- Candy bars

Or present one item for each decade, such as:

- 4 books
- 4 picture frames

On the other hand . . . there are also funny things you can do. To celebrate the 40th birthday of one of our staff members, her "friends" developed a little bio about her and distributed it to all the people in the building.

We're Celebrating
Barb's 40th Birthday

History
Mother of Kayla
Daughter of Anne & Clarence
Sister of Bud, Patti, Susan, Kathy, and Gail

Education
Lawton High School
Parsons Business School

Work Experience
21 years at the Voc-Tech Center

Best Part of Her Job
Finger printing cute men

Favorite Expression
Buzz Off

Color Fetish
Orange phones

Nickname
Barbie or Babs

Pet Peeve
"Don't touch my hair!"

Favorite Color
Teal

Most Embarrassing Moment
"People notice my hairy toes!"

Favorite Animal
Rabbit

Hobbies & Collections
Avon, Dreamsicles, *People* magazine

Most Watched TV Shows
ER, Chicago Hope, Seinfeld, Friends, Days of Our Lives

Recreational Activities
Movies, eating out, camping, hockey, Detroit Tigers' baseball *(except this year)*

(Barbara Coombs, Lawton, MI)

Monthly Birthday Wall Calendar

Make a huge monthly wall calendar. Put each staff member's name or picture on the day that represents his or her birthday. Celebrate the staff members who have birthdays that month at a group meeting. Prepare cookies, cake, ice cream bars, or other special treats. Administrators may also give postcards with an attached gift certificate from a fast food restaurant. Other small gifts may be given to the birthday celebrant. Logo or other items that can be used at work are beneficial to all, e.g., calendars, clocks, notepads, key rings, picture frames, etc.

Sunday	Monday	Tuesday	Wednesday	Thursday	Friday	Saturday
MARCH				1	2	3
4	5	6	7 Susan Garcia	8	9	10
11	12 Karen Obreiterly	13	14	15	16	17 St. Patrick's Day
18	19	20	21	22	23 Marty Summer	24
25 Diane Hodges	26 Kristan Hassed	27	28	29	30	31

Monthly Birthday Celebrations

Make a calendar of birthdays. All birthdays are celebrated on one day of the month—often at a staff meeting. One or more people are assigned to plan the celebration. The way the birthdays are celebrated is up to the planner(s). It could be by having breakfast tacos, pizza, cake and ice cream, an ice cream sundae or cone, etc.

Designer Cards

Hold a contest in which students design a birthday card and the winner receives a $25 cash award. Have the Board of Education and administrators send these cards to the staff on their birthdays. You could also include a certificate for a free cafeteria lunch. *(Saugatuck Public Schools, Saugatuck, MI)*

RESIGNATION OR RETIREMENT

Special people leave their jobs for a variety of reasons and are missed. Recognition of the contributions they made and the friendships they established is important. Some organizations honor *all retiring employees* at an annual event.

- In one school district, all retirees for the year are honored with a banquet. Each school prepares a kind, often humorous statement about the retirees from their school. A spotlight follows the honorees from their seats to the podium, where they receive a certificate of appreciation for service, a crystal clock, and applause from friends and family. *(Fulton County Schools, Atlanta, GA)*

- Snapshots are taken each year at a retirement dinner and put in a photo album along with a copy of the program for an historical document. *(Saline Area Schools, Saline, MI)*

- A printed book is given at a reception honoring the retirees—with information about each retiree, including the date of their retirement, years of service, and a summary of his or her career.

Gifts that other organizations have presented include:

- A school bell *(Lapeer Community Schools, Lapeer, MI)*
- A marble clock with a brass plate engraved with the employee's name and years of service *(Imlay City Community Schools, Imlay City, MI)*
- A brass engraved "A+" plaque *(Allegan Public Schools, Allegan, MI)*
- An engraved golden apple for certified staff and an engraved crystal clock for support staff. *(Saline Area Schools, Saline, MI)*

There are also many ways in which *individuals* who are retiring or leaving can be honored other than holding a group recognition activity.

Monthly Rememberance

Arrange for a plant or flowers to be sent to the retiree each month for the first year of retirement. The greenery can be sent on a specific day of the month such as the date of the monthly Board of Education meeting or other monthly event that the district has.

Postcards

Give each person attending the farewell event a stamped postcard addressed to the person who is leaving. Ask them to write a message on the card and mail it sometime in the next year. Those cards coming in throughout the year will be appreciated. You could also give out postcards made from card stock and have the senders draw pictures on them or paste on a cartoon, photo, etc.

Memory Book

When you mail out the invitations for a retirement celebration, include a card on which people can write a message or share a memory. Have the guests bring the cards to the party and put them into a Memory Book or insert them into a Rolodex holder. *(Kalamazoo Regional Education Service Agency, Kalamazoo, MI)*

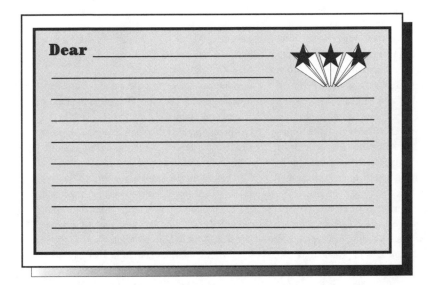

Governor's Proclamation

Contact the governor's office to obtain a proclamation to be read at the retirement event. Frame it for the retiree to display. *(Fulton County Schools, Atlanta, GA)*

Lifetime "Acheesement" Award

If it's a boss who is retiring, hold a wine and cheese reception for "The Big Cheese." Present a Lifetime "Acheesement" Award and acknowledge the person's many years of accomplishments.

Biography

Compile a photographic and written biography of the retiree. It can be used at the retirement celebration as a handout or as part of a printed event program. *(Northwestern Middle School, Alpharetta, GA)*

BIOGRAPHY

John P. Spindler

Northwestern Middle School Principal, John P. Spindler, graduated from Marietta College in 1958 as a speech and drama major with a minor in English education. He began teaching high school English, speech and drama in suburban Cleveland, Ohio. After moving to New Jersey in 1960, he worked as a language arts/reading teacher in a K-8 school and completed his Masters degree in school administration from LeHigh University. After a move to Florida in 1968, Mr. Spindler enrolled in advanced graduate education in middle school curriculum and instruction and later achieved a Specialist degree from the University of Florida in 1979. While in Gainesville, he was District Director of Language Arts and Reading instruction and later became a middle school principal for 17 years. He came to Fulton County in 1987 as Executive Director of Middle Schools and remained at that position until 1996 when he chose to open the new Northwestern Middle School as Principal.

Mr. Spindler has been an officer in the National Middle School Association and served as president of both the Georgia Middle School Association and the Florida League of Middle Schools. He is in high demand as a resource consultant throughout the country in middle grades education. He served as middle school consultant for American Schools in Dhahran, Saudi Arabia, in 1991. He was on-site shortly after Desert Storm establishing middle schools for that country.

John Spindler has written articles for many professional publications over the years. He has produced a film strip: "Lincoln Middle School: Theory Into Practice" and a videotape: "So You Want to Start a Middle School" (1987).

Mr. Spindler has starred in a variety of musicals through participation in the Gainesville Community Playhouse (Florida) including "Carousel," "Oklahoma!," "South Pacific," and "Annie, Get Your Gun."

John Spindler has three children: Greg, Lynn and Marc and is married to Dr. Daun Dickie. He retires from Northwestern and his career in education in the summer of 2000.

Letters of Affirmation

Obtain letters from students, colleagues, parents, etc., about the retiree and read selected letters at the retirement ceremony. *(Northwestern Middle School, Alpharetta, GA)*

FAREWELL GIFTS

Communication Tools

Compile a box of communication tools—a roll of stamps, stationery, computer paper, envelopes, address list, prepaid phone card, etc. Encourage the person to "keep in touch."

Diane Hodges, Author

Car Travel Kit

Make a travel kit that includes jumper cables, a first aid kit, a road atlas, a flashlight, CDs, books-on-tape, coupons to franchise restaurants, a subscription to a travel magazine, a fanny pack, a bed-and-breakfast guide, film, etc.

Geographic Gifts

If the person is moving from the area, give gifts that are symbolic of the place he or she is leaving. When I moved from Austin, I received Texas-related items from all who attended, including a coffee table book, key chain, paper weight, coffee mug, Christmas decoration, barbecue sauce, and coupon for ribs to be shipped anywhere.

Subscriptions

Purchase yearly subscriptions to the *Wall Street Journal*, *USA Today*, *Fortune*, *Money*, *Travel and Leisure*, etc., to be delivered to the retiree's home.

Poetic Good-byes

Good-byes come from both directions. One of our staff members left the department and gave us her departing message in verse form.

Dear School-to-Career

(to the tune of "Home on the Range")

Oh, give me a job
That I am proud of,
Where they always have room for
   one more,
Where the people are neat,
And there's lots good to eat,
And you never have time to get bored!

School, School-to-Career!
Where the dear Career Specialists play,
Where the bosses are smart, and we all
   do our part
To make STC better each day!

Oh, give me a staff
Who knows how to laugh,
Even when things get crazy and stressed.
Because around here
Things are crazy all year,
And you don't ever get time to rest!

School, School-to-Career,
Where the secretaries all dream!
Although we are few, STC will come
   through,
Because everyone works as a team!!!

Oh, give me a desk
Where there isn't a risk
That I have much more room than I need.
Where I won't have a fit
If it's enlarged a bit
Just as long as they wait 'til I leave!

School, School-to-Career,
Oh, what wonderful people are here.
So thanks to you all, 'cause I've just
   had a ball,
As I leave you I'm shedding a tear!!

(Shannon Pearce, Austin, TX)

Looking Forward to Monday Morning

Personal Cards

It was a shock for me not to have a business card when I retired. Have cards printed with the retiring person's name, address, phone number, and e-mail address. The name of the person's spouse may also be included. These cards will come in handy when meeting new people.

Remembrance Gifts

Rather than giving the retiring individual a gift, give a remembrance in the person's name, e.g., a student scholarship, a tree planted on the grounds with a name plaque, a garden planted and named after the individual, etc.

Parting "Gifts" for Colleagues

When I retired and moved out of state, I found I had a lot of "stuff" to get rid of before I left. I showed up at my farewell celebration with a huge box of gift-wrapped items. After I was presented with my retirement gifts, I told my colleagues that I wanted each of them to have a remembrance of me. Each selected an item from the box. They opened their packages one at a time and shared their "treasures" with the group. The items were canned goods from my cupboards, picture frames, cleaning supplies, and so forth. We had a great time, and I had less to pack.

THINK SPRING!

Tailgate Party

At lunch hold a tailgate party in the parking lot to celebrate being able to go outside and enjoy good weather again.

Garden Ingredients

If you live in a part of the country that has cold, snowy winters, you know how people look forward to the coming of spring. Copy these instructions, attach a packet of flower or vegetable seeds, and give them to each staff member.

OUR GARDEN

Plant three rows of **peas.**

Peas of mind
Peas of heart
Peas within yourself

Plant four rows of **squash.**

Squash gossip
Squash selfishness
Squash grumbling
Squash indifference

Plant three rows of **lettuce.**

Lettuce be kind
Lettuce listen to others
Lettuce care about each other

No garden should be without **turnips.**

Turnip to help one another
Turnip the music and dance

To finish our garden we must have **thyme.**

Thyme for fun
Thyme for rest
Thyme for family
Thyme for yourself

Water freely with patience and cultivate with love.
There is much fruit in our garden because you
    reap what you sow.

(Adapted from original version, author unknown)

Looking Forward to Monday Morning

Chapter 8
Celebrating Holidays

HOLIDAY CALENDAR

This is a starter list of celebration dates that are recognized in the United States. Add others as you wish and put them on your yearly calendar.

January 1	New Year's Day
February 14	Valentine's Day
April 1	April Fool's Day
April 22	Earth Day
April—4th Wednesday	Secretary's Day
May 1	May Day
May 5	Cinco de Mayo
May—2nd Sunday	Mother's Day
May—last Monday	Memorial Day
June—3rd Sunday	Father's Day
July 4	Independence Day

August—1st Sunday . . . . Friendship Day

September—1st Monday . . . . Labor Day

September—Sunday after . . . . . . Grandparents'
    Labor Day   Day

October 16 . . . . Boss' Day

October—3rd Saturday . . . . Sweetest Day

October 31 . . . . Halloween

November 11 . . . . Veterans Day

November—4th Thursday . . . . . . Thanksgiving

November or December . . . . 1st day of
                                    Hanukkah

December 25 . . . . Christmas

 ## VALENTINE'S DAY

Valentines Match

Make Valentine's Day hearts in a quantity equal to half the number of people on your staff. Cut the hearts into two pieces, each in a unique way.

Attach half of each heart to a sheet on which the following instructions in verse form are printed, and put them in all staff members' mailboxes. During the day they are to find the staff member who has the half of the heart that matches theirs. At the end of the day, the pairs can come to the office to receive a special treat (e.g., chocolate heart candy).
(W.B. Travis High School, Austin, TX)

Looking Forward to Monday Morning

Valentines Match

Good morning, dear friends. Happy Valentine's Day.

We hope you slept well and are ready to play.

We should recognize that we need one another,

Our hearts aren't complete without sharing together.

Attached is a heart, cut in a way

That you must find its match by the end of the day.

We'll all wear our hearts in hopes we will find

That one special person who's one of a kind.

Bring both matching halves to the office to see

The treat we will give you. It's special—and FREE.

EASTER

Egg Hunt

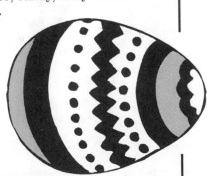

Place positive or motivational quotes, candy, early release coupons, etc., inside plastic eggs or tape them to real hard-cooked eggs. Hide the eggs in various locations for staff members to find. Make sure they are hidden in places the staff frequent so the students don't beat them to it—or you have eggs that aren't found for weeks.

HALLOWEEN

Phantom Ghost

In this activity, a "phantom ghost" delivers treats to celebrate Halloween. Each "ghost" is responsible for delivering treats to two other people. All those participating display a phantom picture on their room or office door. Having a master list of participants is also helpful. The ghosts are not assigned specific participants to deliver treats to, so on the day of delivery they have to keep going to offices where treats have not already been left. Logistically, you could use staff mailboxes as the delivery center for the treats.

Goood . . . Eve . . . ning!

On Halloween Day . . .

The Phantom Ghost
Is coming to town
To leave you some goodies,
I hope you're around.
If you don't wish a spell
Upon you to fall,
Continue this greeting—
the "Phantom call."

First . . .

Post this Phantom
Where it can be seen
And leave it there
Until Halloween.
This ghost will scare
Other Phantoms who
    visit.
Be sure you join in
For a time that's exquisite.

Second . . .

On the day of delivery
[Set the day for the Phantom to strike;
    likely on Halloween.]
Make it quick.
Leave two treats at doors
Where no Phantom has hit.
(If there are two treats already delivered, go on
    to other rooms. Everyone needs deliveries.)

Deliver at dark,
When there is no light.
Leave the goodies and run.
Stay out of sight!!

Last, but not least,
    Come join in the season.
        Don't worry, be happy.
            You need no good reason.
                Be cool, have fun,
                    Be sure not to be seen.
                        Come share in the spirit
                            Of Halloween!

Secret Ghost

Two weeks prior to Halloween, send out a notification to staff of the upcoming "Secret Ghost" activity to determine those who want to participate. Each participant writes his or her name on a piece of paper and places it in a plastic pumpkin container. Each person draws a name from the pumpkin to find what staff member he or she will be the Secret Ghost for. During the week before Halloween, participants anonymously engage in activities that

Secret Ghost

Halloween is almost here
So let's set out to spread some cheer.
On *Wednesday,* start with just a *card.*
Now surely that won't be too hard.

On *Thursday,* brighten up the room.
A *decoration* should lift the gloom.
On *Friday,* bring a little treat—
Something *edible* and fun to eat.

On *Monday,* there's a *pumpkin* theme—
Pretty simple, it would seem.
On *Tuesday,* bring a scary *witch*
To complete your task without a glitch.

At half-past three we'll end the fun
By trying to guess who's the guilty one.
Can you pick the ghost that has been concealed?
On Tuesday, all will be revealed.

*(Jeri Rohl,
Decatur, MI)*

involve giving small items to the person whose name they drew in accordance with the following themes: *a card, a decoration, something edible, something with a pumpkin, and a witch.* Items can appear in the recipient's mailbox, on his or her desk, be delivered by another staff person, pinned to a bulletin board, etc. At the end of the week, all participants are assembled to give the last item on the list and find out the identity of their Secret Ghost. Before revealing the information, let staff members try to guess who their Secret Ghost was and see if they're correct.

Note: The order of the days will vary, depending on which day of the week Halloween falls. In the verse shown, Halloween is on a Tuesday, so activities run Wednesday through Tuesday. *(Jeri Rohl, Decatur, MI)*

Pumpkin Exchange or Giving

Carving pumpkins can be a fun team activity to have in lieu of a staff meeting . . .

OR

People can participate in a Pumpkin Exchange. Each person carves a pumpkin for a person whose name was selected . . .

OR

You can surprise someone with a carved pumpkin with a note attached.

Bill Warren
South Haven, MI

Happy Halloween

You probably haven't had time to carve a pumpkin, and no Halloween is complete without one. So here's one especially for you. I hope you enjoy it. I've left some matches, so light the candle inside, turn out the lights, and enjoy the sight.

Looking Forward to Monday Morning

CHRISTMAS

Secret Santa

This annual event is always fun! As with the Secret Ghost activity, draw names and follow the guidelines for gifts to be given each day. You may want to put a price limit on the gifts, e.g., a maximum of $3 per day for Monday through Thursday and $10 for Friday. I have found that sometimes staff members get carried away with their purchases and it makes the group uncomfortable. Setting limits equalizes the purchases. Each day, the participants secretly deliver their gifts to the person whose name they drew. At the end of the week, everyone meets together to exchange the final gift. Each person guesses who their Secret Santa is and shares the clues he or she picked up during the week.

Holiday Memo

To: All Staff Members
Date: Late November (after Thanksgiving)
Re: Secret Santa

It's that time of the year again! We need to begin planning for Secret Santa week. The scheduled date for this event is the week of _____. For those of you who are not familiar with the Secret Santa procedures, the following is a brief description of what it involves:

1. First, we draw names (only those indicating they want to participate are included).

2. Beginning Monday, December _____ , you discreetly give your Secret Santa one gift each day. (Monday through Thursday will have a theme suggesting the type of gift to give.) Gifts should range in price from $ .50 to $3 per day.

3. On Friday, you bring a gift (maximum cost of $10) for your person and we meet as a group (potluck lunch) and guess who our Secret Santa is.

Themes for Secret Santa Week

Monday	Decoration Day
Tuesday	Naughty or Nice
Wednesday	Goodie Day
Thursday	Musical Day
Friday	Meet Your Secret Santa

Continue the memo with procedures on how to be included in the Secret Santa event and when the drawing of names will be held. Directions for the Secret Santa event can be distributed in poem form as shown:

Secret Santa

Monday—Decoration
'Tis the season to be jolly,
Adorn with mistletoe and holly.
A gift to decorate a tree?
Nay, just one to decorate thee.

Tuesday—Naughty or Nice
Day one is over, the second is here,
Continue on with the season's good cheer.
This day's theme is "naughty or nice."
Which shall it be? I needn't think twice.

Wednesday—Goodies
Candy and cookies, baked goods galore,
Any way possible we could want more?
Days so filled with yummies and sweets,
Let us partake of holiday treats.

Thursday—Music
Music, the gift by no means the least,
Brings joy amidst our merriment and feast.
Listen to the melodies of this season
Praising the holiday's reason.

Friday—General
Gifts we give to those so dear,
Friends and loved ones far and near.
To give others a holiday lift,
We select for them a small Christmas gift.

(Bill Warren, South Haven, MI)

Looking Forward to Monday Morning

Secret Santa

Christmas time is here once more.
It's time to make our spirits soar!
To jolly old Santa we'll lend a hand
By helping to make this Christmas grand.

A **decoration** for **Monday** will start the week.
Make it one at which all can peek.
On **Tuesday,** Santa's gift will be
An **ornament** for your Christmas tree.

To help us get over **Wednesday's** hump
An **edible gift** makes saliva glands pump.
On **Thursday,** Santa will not go wrong
If the gift he brings is a **Christmas song.**

On **Friday,** it's time to round out the game
By deciding on whom to place the blame.
At lunch we'll all bring a nice **final gift**
To give each other a holiday lift.

(Jeri Rohl, Decatur, MI)

Secret Santa

(Gifts are selected to match the song titles each day.)

"Frosty the Snowman" will start us off right.
With Frosty, our **Monday** should be a delight.
On **Tuesday,** we'll hearken as Christmas bells ring
And **"Jingle Bells"** prompts us to let ourselves sing.

"O, Christmas Tree" is the choice for mid-week,
So on **Wednesday** we shouldn't have far to seek.
Thursday's selection will surely spread cheer.
You guessed it! It's **"Rudolph the Red-Nosed Reindeer."**

On **Friday** we're ready to round out the fun.
After five days of gifting, this game will be done.
With **"Santa Claus is Coming to Town"**
Our Christmas adventure will finally wind down.

At lunchtime on **Friday** we'll have a good time
Completing the game that began with this rhyme.
Who had your name? At last you will see.
Your final chance . . . Take a guess. Who will it be?

(Jeri Rohl, Decatur, MI)

Singers' names are a take-off on the name of the staff person who sang the song on the tape.

When one group tried this, staff members were very creative with their gifts. For example, on the fourth day, "Musical Day," one person made a tape for his Secret Santa friend, Susan. He had staff members sing and record songs that had the name "Sue," "Susie," "Susanna," or "Susan" in the title. A list of the Top 10 Susan Songs accompanied the tape.

Top 10 Susan Songs

#10 Susan Took Me Down
Sung by Dr. D. D. Mason

#9 If You Knew Susie
Sung by Little Kitty Kate

#8 Susan, I'm Wasting My Time
Sung by Koola Kel

#7 Oh Susanna
Sung by Dynamic Duo

#6 Peggy Sue
Sung by Late Bloomer

#5 Wake Up, Little Susie
Sung by Pop-Rock Patty

#4 A Boy Named Sue
Sung by Jonny Richardson

#3 Susie Q
Sung by the Fender-Mender

#2 Susie Darling
Sung by Rock-Olu

#1 Run Around Sue
Sung by You Know Who

Looking Forward to Monday Morning

Variation: A variation of the Secret Santa game that I like the best is to give the person a toy on the final day. The toy is personalized to reflect the person's interests, e.g., animals, cooking, etc. These toys are then donated to organizations such as Toys for Tots or the Salvation Army.

HOLIDAY GIFTS & EXCHANGES

The holidays lend themselves to sharing with others. Here are some ideas for activities.

Tree of Love

Through a human services agency, domestic violence safe house, church, or school, identify families who need assistance. Obtain their particular needs and sizes. Write a description of each of the items to be collected on a star, angel, or other paper ornament, e.g., "9-year-old boy—toy" or "12-year-old girl—size 4 casual shoes." Place the ornaments on the tree. Have staff members remove an ornament from the tree and purchase the corresponding gift. Wrap the gift and tape the ornament to the package to identify the contents.

Tree of Warmth

Place an untrimmed tree in a frequently visited place. Have staff members bring in new hats, gloves, mittens, and scarves and hang them on the tree. When the tree is full, donate the warm items to an organization that will give them to people in need.

Food/Toy Drive

Rather than give gifts to each other, have a food and toy drive to prepare baskets and presents for needy families. Have a contest by department, grade level, building, etc.,

for the most items collected. As a group, deliver the baskets to the families. This is a very rewarding experience for everyone involved.

Cookie Exchange

Finding time for holiday baking is often difficult. Have a cookie exchange in which people bake five dozen of their favorite cookies. Meet for a social time and divide the cookies so each person goes home with five dozen assorted types of cookies. Each person provides copies of the cookie recipe to the others in the group.

Staff Gift Exchange

Have a yearly gift exchange with a different gift theme designated each year. Themes you might consider include:

- Crazy coffee mugs
- Calendars
- Holiday CDs
- Holiday ornaments/decorations that correspond to the person's interests, e.g., computers, sports, reading, etc.
- Musical items
- T-shirts
- Books

 "WHITE ELEPHANT" EVENTS

During the holidays people often receive gifts they don't really like or want. What do you do with them? Why not organize a gift exchange or auction?

"White Elephant" Exchange

Have a staff luncheon that culminates with a white elephant gift exchange. Each person brings in a wrapped item they

 Looking Forward to Monday Morning

received as a gift and are thankful to part with—stinky cologne, an ugly tie, fruitcake, etc. Each participant draws a number to determine who picks items first, second, and so on. As each gift is selected, it's unwrapped for all to see.

Variation: When the person opens the gift, he or she may keep it or trade it for someone else's gift. The trade may only occur once, and the person must surrender his or her gift if a trade is requested. People drawing first, when there are no items to trade for, have an opportunity to trade at the end of the drawing.

"White Elephant" Silent Auction

Have each person bring in one or more (set a limit on the number) unwrapped, unwanted but usable items. Display all the items in the lounge or other common area. A silent auction bid sheet accompanies each item. Staff members write in their names and bids next to items they wish to purchase. As the bid is increased, people must continue to rebid, and the highest bidder at the end of the auction period gets the item. Donate the raised funds to a worthwhile charity or activity.

Minimum Bid is $1.00 and increases in a minimum of 50¢ increments.

Silent Auction

Item Name	Your Name	Bid

STAFF GIFTS

It's often a struggle deciding what to give a large staff as a holiday gift that has meaning and is also within your personal budget. Here are some suggestions:

After Thanksgiving, give each staff member a packet or roll of holiday wrapping paper. You beat the holiday rush and your thoughtfulness stands out more. It's also a gift that everyone will use.

Give each person a candy cane with a personalized self-esteem enhancer attached, e.g., "Your smile brightens everyone's day," "Your kindness toward others is marvelous," "Your enthusiasm is contagious," etc.

Prepare a staff breakfast or lunch with a sing-along. I once made place mats that summarized some of the things that had happened since the start of the year.

We've had a fun, challenging year. Thank you for your efforts! Enjoy your vacation.
Happy Holidays!

Gifts for Support Staff

Host a staff breakfast potluck and have each person bring in several items that can be put into baskets for the support staff. Have one staff member dress up as Santa and deliver the gifts. *(Traverse Heights Elementary School, Traverse City, MI)*

"Well(ness)-Received" Gifts

Wellness programs are prominent in many places of employment. Gift giving could be consistent with these efforts. Some items to consider are:

- Home blood pressure monitor
- Gift certificate for a massage
- Bicycle helmet or accessories
- Gift certificate for athletic shoes or clothing
- Tuition for smoking cessation classes
- Healthy food cookbooks
- Reflective clothing
- Kitchen scale
- Exercise video tapes
- Books on hiking and cycling tours
- Bathroom scale
- Multivitamins
- Toothbrushes
- First aid kit
- Smoke detector
- Sports bag
- Gift certificates for sports lessons (e.g., golf, tennis)
- Subscription to a health magazine or newsletter

My best friend said I should get in shape. Round is a shape.
—Author unknown

Gifts for the Boss

A holiday gift for the boss is optional, but if you give one, make sure you know his or her likes and dislikes. At one job, I sent my boss an assortment of cheeses each Christmas. Finally, after I'd been doing this for about ten years, he mentioned in a staff meeting that he hated cheese. Ooops! Group gifts are probably the best.

- Holiday wreath
- Gift certificate for a massage
- Coffee or tea assortment
- Book-on-tape if he or she commutes to work
- Scratch pads printed with his or her doodles

HOLIDAY COMMUNICATIONS

Personalized Cards

Staff members draw names and create a holiday card for the person whose name they chose. The opportunity for creativity is endless, e.g., singing cards, candy-decorated cards, original poems, etc. Have a gathering at which these cards are presented.

Memos, Newsletters, Bulletin Boards

Include holiday cartoons in your memos, on the bulletin boards, or in your newsletter.

"We're in trouble. He wants one for Christmas!"

Looking Forward to Monday Morning

"It's a letter from the Energy Commission. They want me to stop giving out coal in favor of a more environmentally friendly material."

"Where's the chimney?"

"Excuse me, folks. Can Blitzen use your bathroom?"

"Stamp out those coals, turkey . . . !"

Collective Holiday Card

Make a collective holiday card in which each person extends a wish to all. It makes a lovely expression of joy.

 # HOLIDAY EVENTS

Wellness Event

Reserve the facilities at a health club for a designated amount of time. Have the staff participate in group activities such as racquetball, basketball, walking, and aerobics and serve healthy snack foods and drinks.

Bowling

Holiday events are such fun. Try a "Strike up the Season" bowling party.

Costume Day

Costumes aren't just for Halloween. Have a holiday dress-up day. Staff members can use their creativity to design an outfit that represents the season, e.g., reindeer, a decorated tree, a gift, and so forth. Judging of costumes is optional.

Looking Forward to Monday Morning

Section IV

Celebrate Yourself

*If you ever need a hand to pat
you on the back, you have one
right at the end of your arm.*

Chapter 9
Appreciate Yourself

SELF-AFFIRMATIONS

Humans need to be recognized and appreciated for who we are and what we do. From time to time, we need to have affirmations of our successes and contributions. We often say to ourselves, *I will never forget this day . . . this feeling . . . these words . . .* but those memories often fade. We need to have reminders of our accomplishments to keep our attitudes positive when we're faced with setbacks. This recognition comes from both internal and external sources. We don't have control over the external sources, but we do have control over ourselves. We can and should appreciate ourselves and the events that occur in our lives. These accomplishments don't have to be monumental; sometimes it's the small victories that can bring us the most joy.

I remember feeling fearful after my divorce. Despite the fact that my father's second career was as a bank vice president, I had never learned how to balance a checkbook. While I was married, that job was relegated to my husband.

Eighteen years later, I was on my own with no clue as to how to balance one. For a year I bartered with my ex-husband: I'd give him a bottle of wine if he'd continue with the reconciliation challenge. One day, I decided that I should be able to figure it out. After all, if I was going to be truly independent, I needed to break this tie. Four hours later, it *balanced*! I was like a kid—I yelled with joy, jumped around the house, called a friend to share my achievement, and told the kids to tell their dad that I had balanced my checkbook.

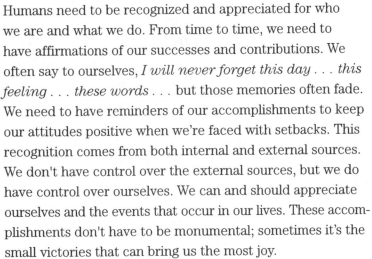

I'm sure no one quite understood the marker event this was in my life, but I knew it was. No one was going to give me an *atta girl,* so I gave myself one. We need to acknowledge our victories and success—no matter how small.

"THE BEST THING ABOUT TODAY WAS" JOURNAL

When my children were young, I loved the time I spent with them before bedtime. I would ask them, *What was the best thing about today?* They would tell me in a sentence or two what it was. It was a good habit to get into because it allowed us to focus on the positive things, and I found myself ending my day with this same process. I encourage you to do the same. At the end of the day, write a one- or two-line entry beginning with, *The best thing about today was . . .* Remember, the events don't have to be monumental— celebrate your small victories and things that made you happy. Then, on the days when you feel unappreciated or that nothing good happens in your life, pull out your journal and review the previous month's entries. This simple act can change your attitude for the better.

Here are some examples:

- I balanced my checkbook! Yes!
- I saved $15 on groceries by using coupons.
- My son left me a note in the kitchen that ended with *I love you, Mom.*
- My brother called today. (Brothers are wonderful.)
- I cleaned off a corner of my desk today. Now, on to the next pile.
- I have clean sheets tonight. They feel great.
- I had shelves installed in my closet and the installer said I was the nicest person he had ever worked with. That made me feel good.
- I completed three things on my "To Do" List.
- I had lunch with my friend.

- I received a thank-you note from an employee that read, *I can't remember a time that you have not had a smile on your face and a pleasant word to say. The district would benefit from having more people like you.* **(See the form at the back of this book to order a journal.)**

September

The best thing about today was…

1 _____
2 _____
3 _____
4 _____
5 _____
6 _____
7 _____
8 _____
9 _____
10 _____

What makes you feel really good?

- Running through sprinklers
- Laughing for no reason at all
- Friends
- A bubble bath
- Hot towels right out of the dryer
- Swinging on swings
- Making chocolate chip cookies
- Watching a sunrise
- Hearing a baby giggle

- Playing with a puppy
- Waking up and going back to sleep again
- The beach
- Overhearing a nice comment about yourself
- Good dreams
- Getting mail
- **Getting up on Monday morning and knowing you have a job to go to.**

Pat on the Back

Sometimes you deserve a pat on the back, and it doesn't come. When that happens, tape this hand to the wall, lean against it, and give yourself a "pat on the back."

You Deserve It!

SELF-AFFIRMATIONS CORNER

I closed the door of a colleague's office for a confidential conversation. On the back of the door were notes, cards, phone messages, etc., from students, parents, coworkers, and administrators under the heading, *Atta Girl.* She had taped a collection of accomplishments and praises on her door and used them to remind herself that she made a difference in the lives of others and was appreciated. On days when she had her doubts about her career choice and no evidence of her impact on others, she closed the door and read her notes.

PROFESSIONAL PORTFOLIOS

Portfolios are used as a means of obtaining employment and for performance reviews. By definition, they are a collection of items that demonstrate your accomplishments and interests. The contents could include a résumé, previous performance evaluations, notes from the public, students, or parents, newspaper articles, lesson plans, pictures of work-related activities, letters of recommendation, certificates, degrees, awards, etc. Developing a Portfolio is a self-esteem builder. Periodically reviewing it and constantly updating it are motivating, self-renewing activities.

Professional Portfolio

Resumé

Education

Work

Management

Awards

Volunteer

When you create your Portfolio, don't be intimidated by the conditioning you may have received as a child that *bragging* is inappropriate behavior (whenever you said something good about yourself, someone would tell you, *Be quiet—stop bragging*). Change that mind-set and give yourself permission to display and demonstrate the positive things that make you unique.

The staff that I supervised created their Professional Portfolios. Each week when we had a staff meeting, one person presented his or her Portfolio to the group. We learned amazing things about each other. We got to know our coworkers as whole people, not just as colleagues who worked down the hall. *(See the form at the back of this book to order Portfolio materials.)*

YOUR OFFICE ENVIRONMENT

Reward yourself by doing special little things. The environment in which you spend 2,000 hours a year has a great influence on whether you look forward to going to work. Create a place that feels good, makes you feel productive, appreciated, and "fits" you. Make it an inviting place that welcomes you and others every day and where you love spending time.

Colors

Add color wherever you can—paper clips, notebooks, pens, file folders, etc. The colors you use in your work environment will have an effect on how you function and how you feel. There is a psychology to colors that is important to be aware of in your decorating. When you go into restaurants notice how often red is used. Red stimulates a person's glands, which makes customers hungrier and apt to spend more money. Red is a good color to use in rooms used for brainstorming. It also works well in cafeterias and break rooms.

My school had a media center where students rarely sat down to read or look at books. The room was decorated in orange, an uplifting color, but one that promotes movement. It's great for fast food chains—but not for a library. We changed the colors of the room to soft pastels and off white, and it gave the room a more spacious, relaxed feel. Use of the media center and the number of books checked out increased considerably.

If you want to feel . . .	Then decorate in . . .
Calm/relaxed/friendly	Yellow, apricot, and blue
Stable	Green and yellow
Independent	Purple
Sophisticated	Blue and gold
Avant-garde	Black, white, and silver

Lighting

Light can trigger changes in body chemistry and is especially important in combating seasonal blues. People who work with good lighting have been found to perform faster and make fewer mistakes. If you have a window at work, open the blinds. If you don't, bring in extra lamps.

"You" Drawer

Make one of your desk drawers a "you" drawer. Stock it with things that bring you comfort or will help if you are in need. Items to include may be a sewing kit, safety pins, Band-Aids, pain reliever, antacid, cough drops, breath mints, deodorant, mouthwash, make-up or shaving kit, panty hose, neck tie, personal lingerie, a spare set of glasses, greeting cards (birthday, sympathy, get well) for quick responses to situations, $10, and a treat of your choice (chocolate, salty snack, candy bar, etc.). We all have "those days" and knowing that we are prepared and can get through them easily can create a sense of self-confidence and reduce anxiety.

Décor

Decorate your office with items that are important to you. Put a pillow in your chair and decorate your work environment with reminders of accomplishments and positive, motivating things. Frame certificates, hang awards, or make a collage of newsletter articles about your accomplishments and contributions, post notes from internal or external personnel, performance appraisals, photos of mentors, etc. Combat the nagging effect of office memos on your bulletin board by making a motivational display of things that you love. Create a bulletin board of quotes or cartoons that make you smile.

Fragrances

Certain fragrances can help your mood. The part of your brain that responds to smell interacts with the part that regulates emotions. Add potpourri or other aromatic products to your office to give yourself a lift. Use peppermint, jasmine, or lemon to increase your productivity. Rosemary, cloves, spearmint, and nutmeg are also stimulants. To help you relax, chamomile, orange, lavender, pine, and rose may be helpful. Actually, the aromatherapy I like best is the smell of popcorn!

DAILY SCHEDULE

Self-nurturing is important. I have a sign on my desk that says, *If not you, then who?* It reminds me to take care of myself. When scheduling your daily activities, make up a name of a person, e.g., "Maggie Martin," and schedule fifteen minutes for this fictitious visitor. This assures you that fifteen minutes each day will go unscheduled and you can do what you need to do. It may be that you are able to close your door and relax, have a cup of herbal tea, listen to music—whatever you decide. Call it a "Joy Break" or a "Wellness Break." Use the time to read, stretch, or meditate.

Sometimes we need to move away from
The busyness of the world around us
And search out the quiet places—
Places where we may seek understanding.
Take time to organize our thoughts,
And be ready to give all that is asked of us
In our world again.
—Author Unknown

Index —

A

S

Y

Diane Hodges is available to speak on the following topics:

Looking Forward to Monday Morning

Diane Hodges, a former human resources director and school administrator, shares numerous staff appreciation and recognition activities that can be implemented to promote a positive work environment. She presents low-cost, fun ideas that staff members can do at work during meetings, holidays, lunchtime, etc., that help them look forward to coming to work. This presentation helps people make each day a "Funday."

A Résumé is Not Enough to Get the Job You Want

Learn how to "sell yourself" during a job interview or performance review using a Professional Portfolio that documents the skills and experience listed on your résumé. Diane shows you how to create "leave behinds" that will make interviewers remember you. This program is especially helpful for educators who are working with college students or other adult learners who will be entering or re-entering the workforce. An accompanying book, *Your Portfolio: A Visual Résumé*, is available.

The Portfolio: Your Passport to HIRE Education

Success in today's competitive job market requires more than a transcript of student records that are maintained by an educational institution. This program shows educators how to assist students in developing student-managed Portfolios that document their employability skills. Students use the Portfolios in their job or college placement process. Documents students have included in their Portfolios are showcased. An accompanying instructional guide and student workbook are available.

GOT A FUN ACTIVITY?

Do you have low-cost recognition and appreciation activities or other fun things that you do in your workplace? If so, send them to Diane Hodges at Threshold Group (address below) for possible inclusion in a future volume of *Looking Forward to Monday Morning*.

Name _____

Organization _____

Address _____

Phone _____ Fax _____

E-mail _____

THRESHOLD *group*

4991 Concannon Court, San Diego, California 92130
858.509.1913 phone • 858.794.4078 fax
e-mail: threshold3@aol.com • website: www.thresholdgrp.com

"Monday Morning" Products

Item	Item #	Description	Price
	300	**Looking Forward to Monday Morning** • A book filled with staff recognition and appreciation activities and fun things to do at work—all on a low budget. *Also available from Amazon.com*	**$22.00**
	301	**Laugh Lines** • A booklet of Internet humor to be included in memos, posted on a bulletin board or in a lounge, used as a meeting starter, etc., to increase the number of workday laughs, chuckles, and smiles. Keep a supply on hand to give colleagues and friends when they are ill.	**$10.00**
	302	**The Best Thing About Today Was . . . Journal** • A daily journal in which you record the ending of the sentence, "The best thing about today was . . ." It allows you to focus on the small victories and joys of each day. Perfect for first-year staff members.	**$10.00**
	303	**"Credit" Cards (CD)** • 24 cards that express praise, credit, and appreciation of coworkers. Keep them handy to deliver immediately whenever credit is due. *(PC format only)*	**$12.00**
	304	**All-Occasion Cards** • 24 cards for responding to the events in our daily lives: "I'm sorry," "Welcome Back," etc. Keep them handy so that you're always ready with just the right words. *(PC format only)*	**$12.00**

"Monday Morning" Products

Item #		Description	Price
	305	**Survival Kits (diskette)** • A diskette of artwork to prepare *Survival Kits for Every Day, Teachers, and Retirees* to give to coworkers, friends, etc. *(PC format only)*	$6.00
	306	**T-shirt** • A *Looking Forward to Monday Morning* T-shirt. It's perfect for casual dress days. *(Specify size—Men's M, L, XL)*	$15.00
	307	**Combo Package—The Best of Monday Morning** • Contains each of the Items #300, 301, 302, 303, 304, 305, 306, and 105. *(Specify size for T-shirt—Men's M, L, XL)*	$99.00
	308	**Video: "Looking Forward to Monday Morning"** • 1 hour conference presentation of recognition and appreciation activities and fun things to do at work.	$75.00
	105	**Professional Portfolio—"Your Portfolio: A Visual Résumé" and Leather-look Binder** • A detailed description of how to prepare a Portfolio to document your achievements and interest for a job interview or performance appraisal. It's also an excellent tool to help staff members get to know each other better and as a self-esteem builder. Includes a gallery of sample color Portfolio pages. Includes a leather-look 3-ring binder and page protectors.	$30.00

"Monday Morning" Products

Name _____ Title _____

Institution/Organization _____

Address _____

City _____ State _____ ZIP/Postal Code _____ Country _____

Phone _____ Fax _____ E-mail _____

Item #	Qty.	Unit Price	Size	Description	Amount

Subtotal	
Sales Tax	
** S & H	
TOTAL	

*California residents add 7.75% Sales Tax

**Shipping & Handling is 10% of subtotal (min. S&H charge of $6.50)

Method of Payment:

❏ Check
   Payable to Threshold Group.

❏ Purchase Order
   # _____

❏ Credit Card   ❏ MasterCard   ❏ Visa
   Card # _____ Exp. Date _____
   Signature _____

Threshold Group
4991 Concannon Court
San Diego, California 92130
858.509.1913 phone
858.794.4078 fax
e-mail: Threshold3@aol.com